Toys of Early America

...you can make

by

Reba Ann Dunmire

South Holland, Illinois
THE GOODHEART-WILLCOX COMPANY, INC.
Publishers

INTRODUCTION

Memories, love, and Yankee ingenuity are the essence of the toys and pastimes of the children of the early USA.

When early settlers and pioneers left their old homes, there was no space in sailing ships or in covered wagons for toys. But memories do not use space. So it was that recollections of the toys and games that had given them pleasure during their childhood traveled with them. Thus were they preserved to be duplicated again and again.

Imported toys could be purchased in the larger towns. Occasionally, local craftspeople would make them as a sideline. But, primarily, the making of playthings for the children was a family affair.

Since these hardy folks had their roots in many different homelands, old settler toys came from a diverse background. Today's children enjoy these toys as much as their great, great grandparents did. As one fourth grader wrote, ''And the pioneers are smarter then I thought because the toys they play with are fun.''

About the directions

Welcome to the exciting world of making toys from ''scratch.'' Those you will be making are adapted from toys made for early American children.

The few materials and tools required are basic. The novice who is making toys on the dining room table will have no difficulty with the simple instructions. The experienced woodworker, on the other hand, will be able to adapt the instructions to more skillful methods.

Patterns are full size unless otherwise indicated. Do not be afraid to experiment and substitute. That is part of the fun.

Hints, shortcuts, and other good things

1. To save table tops, use an old glass from a picture frame as a cutting board. Bind sharp edges with masking tape.
2. Gesso adds strength to cardboard and will cover a multitude of mistakes.
3. When making small holes with an awl or compass, use a twisting motion as opposed to a jabbing one.
4. While gluing and painting, work on wax paper. Its protective finish rarely sticks to work surface.
5. In most craft techniques, such as painting and gluing, moderation is the key to success. You can always add but you cannot take away!

Copyright 1983

by

THE GOODHEART-WILLCOX CO. INC.

Library of Congress Cataloging in Publication Data

Dunmire, Reba.
Toys of early America you can make.

Summary: Gives instructions and describes the necessary tools and materials for making a variety of traditional toys and games.
1. Toy making.   2. Toys—United States—History.
[1. Toy making. 2. Toys—History. 3. Handicraft]
I. Title.
TT174.D86   1983   745.592   82—24244
ISBN 0—87006—441—X

CONTENTS

BALANCE TOYS

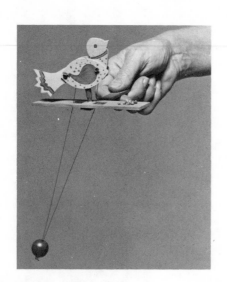

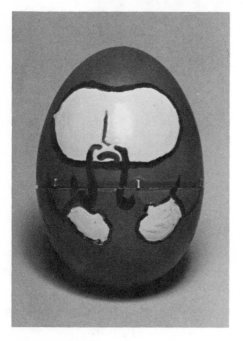

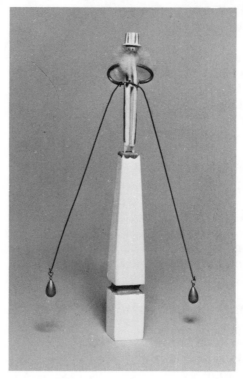

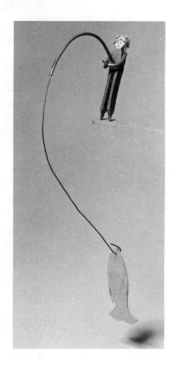

Pecking Bird

A pendulum toy is an action toy, its movement powered by a swinging weight. As the pendulum swings back and forth, the bird pecks away at its corn and its tail goes up and down.

Since the days of the Persian empire and ancient Greece, this kind of toy has pleased children wherever it appeared. The history of its travels from the Mediterranean countries into Europe closely parallels the growth of Old World civilization. During the Dark Ages these toys, probably stowed away in the packs of soldiers and merchants, made their way to Poland and Russia.

The tragedy of the two Childrens' Crusades in 1212 left a deep mark on parents. They turned more to toy making probably in their desire to entertain their children. In France and Germany, woodcarvers produced the pecking bird to the delight of children. Immigrants brought the idea to Pennsylvania.

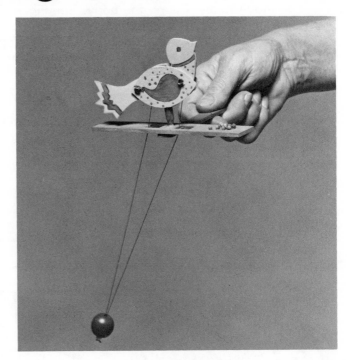

Supplies: Piece of balsa or basswood, 1/8'' x 2'' x 13''; length of heavy-duty button and carpet thread, 24 in. long; three inch length of wire that will hold shape when bent; dowel, 1/4'' x 2''; heavy bead or sinker; white glue; acrylic or model enamel paint; No. 2 pencil; sheet of tracing paper; scrap cardboard, 8'' x 10''; few kernels of corn or grain.

Tools: Craft knife; compass; needlenose pliers; clip clothespins (2); paint and glue brushes.

How to make
1. Using the No. 2 pencil, transfer the full-size patterns onto tracing paper. Place the tracing, face down, on the wood. Be careful to follow the grain lines. Retrace the patterns onto the wood. The wood will pick up the lead from the original tracing. See Fig. 1-A.
2. Using scrap cardboard as a cutting board, cut out the parts with a knife. To reduce the danger of splitting the wood, score the lines first with the knife tip.
3. Make holes indicated in the pattern. Use the point of the compass with a screwing motion. Mark holes ''T'' (for thread) and ''W'' (for wire) as indicated on the drawings. It will avoid mix-ups later.
4. Smooth edges with fine sandpaper.
5. Paint before assembling, if you wish.
6. Glue the handle to the underside of the platform. Clamp with clothespin until the glue dries, Fig. 1-B.
7. Sharpen one end of the dowel to a point. Glue it in the center of the body, Fig. 1-C. Clamp with a clothespin.
8. Cut the 3 in. length of wire in half. Form a spiral on one end of each wire using a pliers. Going from the outside of the body piece with dowel glued on it, insert the wires through holes marked ''W.''
9. Cut the thread in half. Tie one piece through the hole ''T'' in the head and the other piece through the hole ''T'' in the tail. Let the threads hang down.
10. Place the body piece on the table, dowel side up. Place head and tail pieces on the body. Poke wires through ''W'' holes.

11. Put a little glue on the dowel and place the other body on it slipping the wires through the ''W'' holes. Avoid getting glue on the threads.
12. Make loops in the wire ends to hold the body in place. Allow some play so that the head and tail can move freely. Clamp the body. See Fig. 1-D.
13. Fill the hole in the center of the platform with glue. Insert the pointed end of the dowel. Drop threads through the square cutouts in the platform. Allow the glue to dry.
14. Run the threads through the bead. Tie the ends in a knot big enough so it will not slip through the bead. Make sure the threads are the same length. They should extend about 3 in. below the bottom of the platform. See Fig. 1-E.

To use your toy, grasp the handle and move your hand in a horizontal circular motion. The head and tail should go up and down alternately. Glue kernels of corn on the platform where the bird's beak strikes.

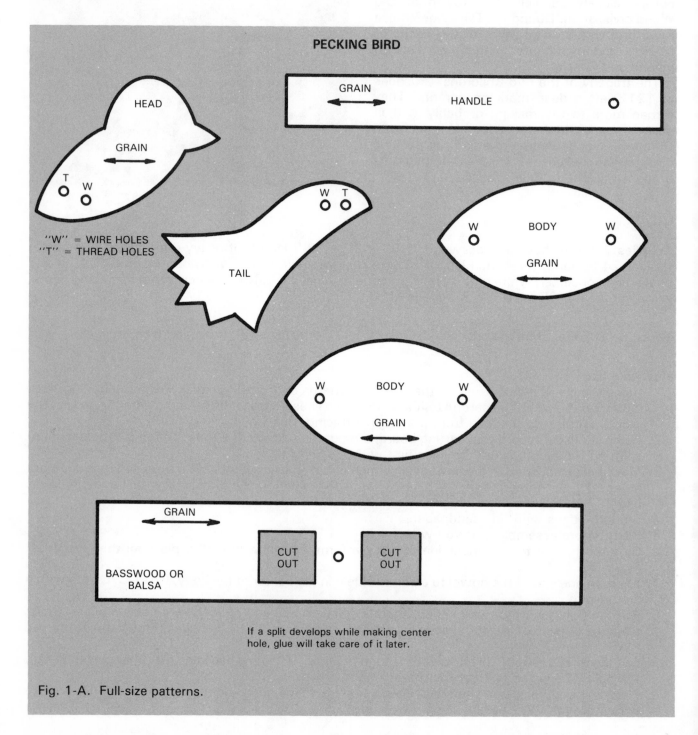

Fig. 1-A. Full-size patterns.

6

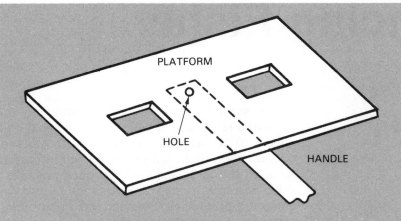

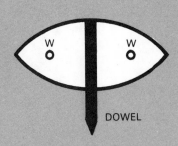

Fig. 1-B. Attaching handle (not to scale).

Fig. 1-C. Gluing dowel to body.

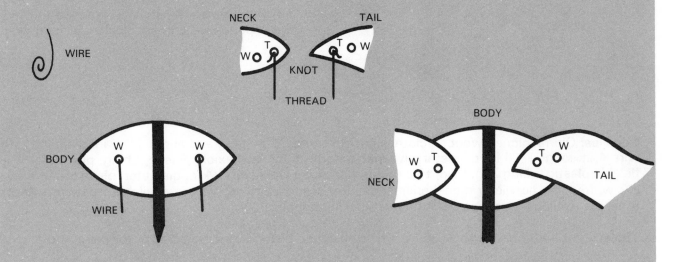

Fig. 1-D. Attach wires and threads.

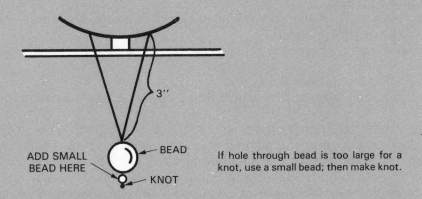

If hole through bead is too large for a
knot, use a small bead; then make knot.

Fig. 1-E. Attaching the bead.

Balancing Fisher

The sight of a toy figure teetering on the edge of a table is incredible, if not magical, to a child. While waiting for the fall that never comes, the child, like his or her counterparts through the ages, asks why it does not fall.

No one country can claim this toy as its own, since the principle of balance has been recognized for thousands of years. It has often been used to entertain. Balance, of course, depends on lowering the center of gravity.

Every culture, ancient as well as modern, has its version of balance toys. A person riding a horse, a sawyer, a hoe boy, and a fisher were all popular toys among settlers in the early 1800s. The toy's "activity" tended to mirror the experiences and occupation of its maker.

Supplies: Old fashioned wooden clothespin; stiff wire 18 in. long and about 1/16 in. diameter; stiff wire 4 in. long, 1/16 in. diameter; five inch length of 1/8 in. flexible plastic tubing; piece of 1/4 in. flexible plastic tubing 2 in. long; two round, flat metal washers, 3/4 in. diameter; piece of felt 4 by 3 in.; white glue; acrylic or model enamel paint in assorted color; (wire is available from craft shops; tubing is available at shops selling model-making supplies).

Tools: Craft knife; drill with 1/16 in. bit; needlenose pliers; scissors; brushes for paint and glue.

How to make

1. Make holes in the clothespin for the balance wire and arms. Drill the balance wire hole through the body front to back 1/4 in. above legs. Drill the arm hole from side to side 1/4 in. below the head. See Fig. 2-A.
2. Using the craft knife, shave the bottom of the legs to a point, Fig. 2-B. Save the shavings for hair.
3. To make the arms, cut the 2 in. piece of 1/4 in. tubing in half. Cut one end of each piece at a slant to fit against the body, Fig. 2-C.
4. Paint all the parts except the wire. The fisherman will need a shirt, trousers, and boots. Paint the arm tubing to look like the sleeves of the shirt.
5. Use the shavings from Step 2 for hair. Spread white glue on the hair area of the head. Glue shavings to the head.
6. Cut two fish from the felt. Use the pattern in Fig. 2-D.
7. Glue them together sandwich style with both washers in the center. Make a small hole for the mouth. See Fig. 2-D.
8. Using pliers, form a small circle (for a hand) on one end of the 4 in. long arm wire. Thread the other end through one arm tube so that the slanted end is against the body. Slide the wire through the body, through the other arm tube. Form another hand. Cut off any excess wire. Put a little glue where the arms join the body. See Fig. 2-E.
9. Thread the 18 in. wire through the longer piece of tubing to make the fishpole. Push the end through the body from front to back. Turn down about 1/2 in. of wire in back to hold it in place. Hook the other end of the wire to the fish's mouth.

10. Curve the balance wire gently so that the fish hangs under the fisher's feet. The toy will now balance on the edge of a table, a fingertip, a pencil, or, perhaps, even on your nose.

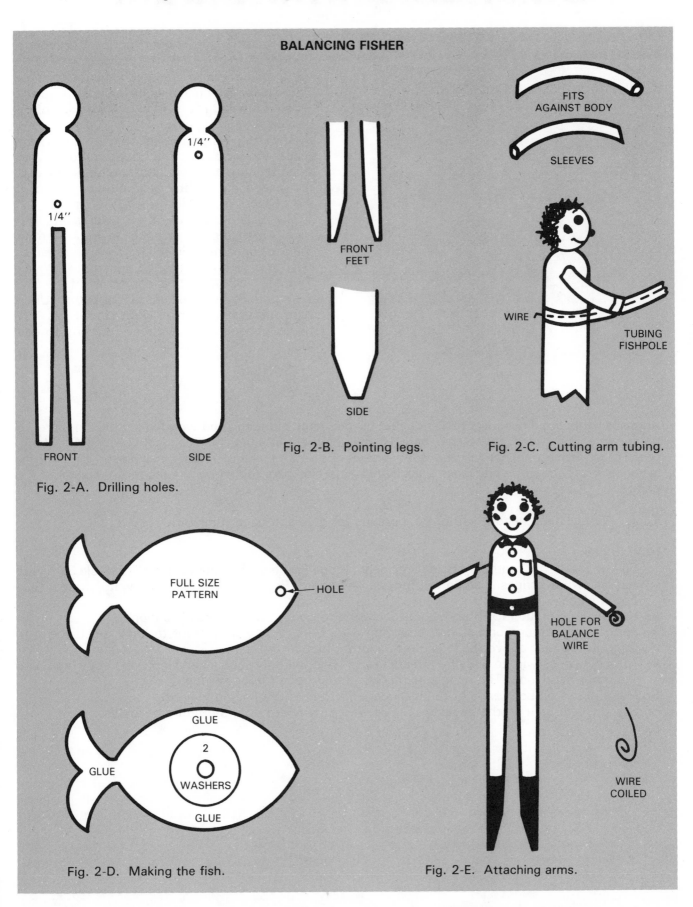

BALANCING FISHER

FITS AGAINST BODY

SLEEVES

1/4''

1/4''

FRONT

SIDE

Fig. 2-A. Drilling holes.

FRONT FEET

SIDE

Fig. 2-B. Pointing legs.

WIRE

TUBING FISHPOLE

Fig. 2-C. Cutting arm tubing.

FULL SIZE PATTERN

HOLE

GLUE

2 WASHERS

GLUE

GLUE

Fig. 2-D. Making the fish.

HOLE FOR BALANCE WIRE

WIRE COILED

Fig. 2-E. Attaching arms.

Balancing Uncle Sam

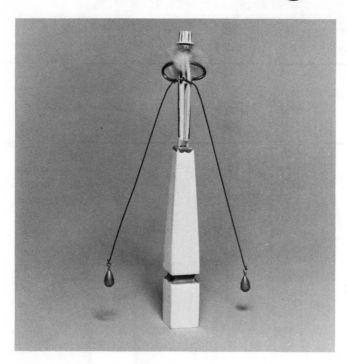

While Americans were fighting the Revolutionary War in 1776, the children of France were being introduced to balance toys. A figure balanced on a pedestal aided by a curved wire with weights on either end was one of the most common types.

After the American Revolution, these toys made their way to this country. Soon, they were being made here. An outstanding example is seen in the Abby Aldrich Rockefeller Folk Art collection at Williamsburg, Virginia.

The balancing man, here, represents Dan Rice, America's first famous clown. A patriotic man, he performed in top hat, whiskers, and a red and white stripped costume. When Thomas Nast, a political cartoonist of the Civil War period, was asked to caricature Uncle Sam, he drew his inspiration from Rice. Incidentally, legend says that President Lincoln was a Dan Rice fan.

Supplies: Unpainted chair leg 7 1/2 in. long for pedestal; old fashioned wooden clothespin; bare 18 gauge wire 18 in. long; two pieces bare 18 gauge wire 4 in. long; flexible plastic tubing 4 in. long; two 1/2 oz. fishing sinkers with loops; absorbent cotton for hair and beard; small plastic top hat (this is sold at craft stores); white glue; black laundry marking pen; red and white model enamel or acrylic paints.

Tools: Wire cutters; needlenose pliers; brushes for glue and paint; drill with 1/16 in. bit.

How to make
1. Follow Steps 1, 2, and 3 for Balancing Fisher (page 8). Paint the figure to look like Uncle Sam with red and white stripes. Use cotton for hair and beard. Paint hat with red and white stripes. Glue hat in place.
2. Use Fisher direction for Step 8 to attach arms to body. Shape hands like loops.
3. Form a loop on one end of the remaining 4 in. wire. Going from front to back, push the wire through the hole above the legs. Form another loop in the rear.
4. Attach balance wire to body by threading the 18 in. wire through a hand loop, the body loop, and the other hand loop. The middle of the wire must be in the body loop.
5. Make hooks on both ends of the balance wire to hold the fishing weights.
6. Stand Uncle Sam on the pedestal. Curve wire downward until the figure balances.

Tumbling Toy

Since the days of Marco Polo, China has been known for its intriguing toys and other products. In the early 1800s, clipper ships, returning from Canton, were laden with silks, fireworks, and other exotic goods. The crews did not forget their children at home. Toys were often among the contents of their sea chests. This is how topple toys invaded Europe and America.

These ingenious little figures were able to topple head over heels down an incline or steps. The original toys depicted acrobats. Based on the principle of a shifting center of gravity, they contained a tube of mercury concealed in the body of the dolls. As the mercury slid from one end to the other the dolls went end over end as if in defiance of gravity.

Topple toys were an instant success. This led to many variations. Our toy is based on a toppling cardboard tablet made by and for Victorian era children.

Supplies: Sheet of balsa wood, 7 3/4'' x 2 3/4'' x 3/16''; two kitchen matchboxes, 4 3/4'' x 4'' x 2 1/2''; safety matchbox; masking tape, 3/4'' wide; white glue; clip clothespins; acrylic gesso; poster board, 8'' x 10''; large marble about 3/4'' diameter; sheet of white construction paper; model enamel or acrylic paints; tracing paper; pencil.

Tools: Craft knife; scissors; brushes for applying glue, gesso, and paint.

How to make

1. Remove the drawer from one kitchen matchbox. Save it to use as a storage drawer. Cut the other kitchen matchbox in half. Remove the drawer from one half. Turn it over and slide it into the other half section to form a cube, Fig. 4-A. With masking tape, seal edges of all but the full-size kitchen matchbox.
2. Stack boxes to make steps as shown in Fig. 4-B. Glue together. Clamp where possible while glue dries. Seal new joints with masking tape.
3. Coat the entire step assembly with gesso. Trim 1/8 in. from top of drawer removed in Step 1. Paint ends and inside of drawer with gesso. Give a second coat of gesso and allow to dry. Paint with enamel or acrylic paints.
4. Trace the pattern for the top and bottom of the tumbling box. See Fig. 4-C. Transfer to poster board and cut out.
5. The side of the box is made from a strip of poster board 1 in. wide and 6 1/2 in. long. Before laying out the side, first test the poster board by gently bending it. Hold it by one edge and then an adjacent edge to see which way the ''grain'' of the paper runs. It bends easier parallel to the grain. The length of the strip should be layed out across the grain so it can be bent around the box.
6. Place a strip of masking tape on the long edges of the side strip. Let half its width hang off the edge. Slash the tape at 1/4 in. intervals up to the edge of the cardboard, Fig. 4-D. This will help it fold over the curved edges of top and bottom without buckling.
7. Attach the side to the bottom by rolling the side around the bottom folding the slashed edge of the tape onto the outside of the bottom to hold it in place. Tape down the overlap. Turn the open end up and put the large marble inside.

8. Fold back the masking tape away from the opening. Put top in place so it rests on top of the taped side. Fold the masking tape down over the top. See Fig. 4-E.
9. Paint the box with gesso. Let it dry.
10. Transfer the clown pattern onto construction paper. Do the same with the pattern for the end pieces. Cut out and color them. Glue them onto the box. (This was a common method of decorating toys of yesteryear.) Coat the whole box with white glue. It will dry clear, providing a durable surface.

To make the clown tumble:

Stand the clown on end at the top of the steps. It will tumble down. If you turn the steps over you will have an incline which works just as well. Store the clown in the drawer left in the larger matchbox.

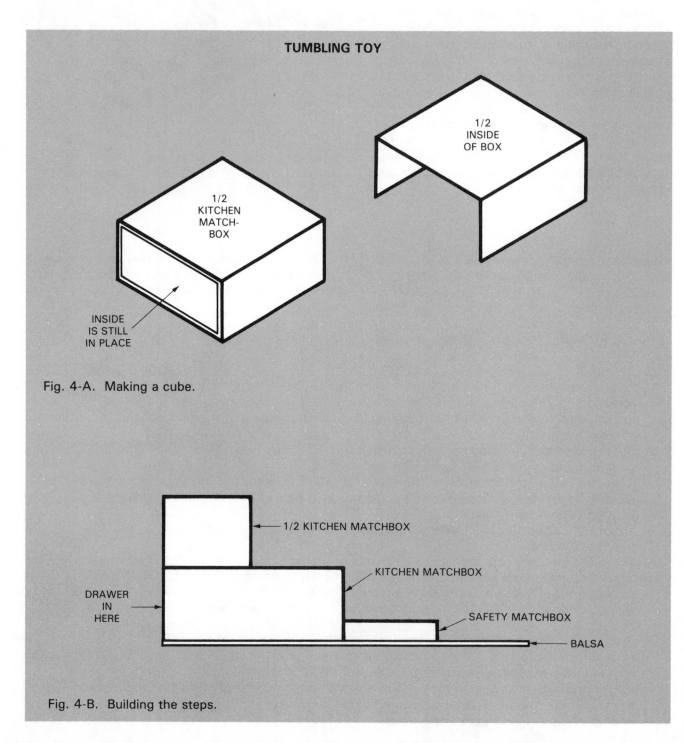

TUMBLING TOY

1/2 INSIDE OF BOX

1/2 KITCHEN MATCH- BOX

INSIDE IS STILL IN PLACE

Fig. 4-A. Making a cube.

1/2 KITCHEN MATCHBOX

KITCHEN MATCHBOX

DRAWER IN HERE

SAFETY MATCHBOX

BALSA

Fig. 4-B. Building the steps.

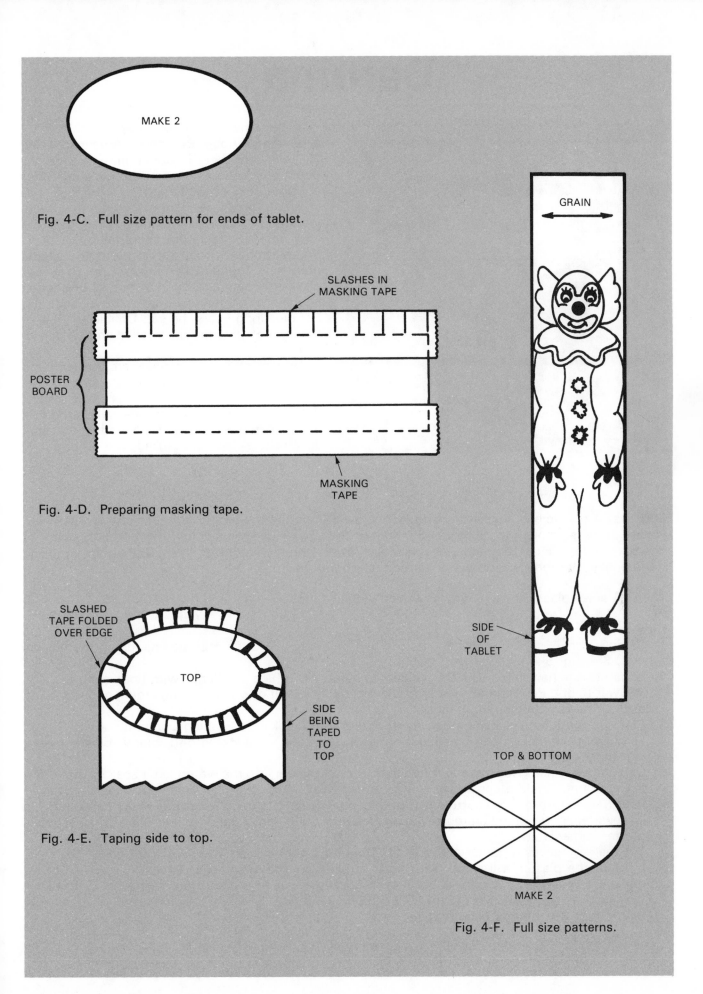

MAKE 2

Fig. 4-C. Full size pattern for ends of tablet.

SLASHES IN
MASKING TAPE

POSTER
BOARD

MASKING
TAPE

Fig. 4-D. Preparing masking tape.

SLASHED
TAPE FOLDED
OVER EDGE

TOP

SIDE
BEING
TAPED
TO
TOP

Fig. 4-E. Taping side to top.

GRAIN

SIDE
OF
TABLET

TOP & BOTTOM

MAKE 2

Fig. 4-F. Full size patterns.

13

Daruma

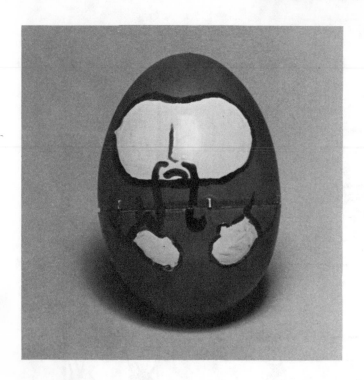

A German Putzelmann, a Japanese Ok-tok-I, a French La Poussah, and an American Kelly, all have one thing in common. They are the direct descendents of the Daruma, a centuries old tilting toy of the Orient.

Tilting toys are figures having a curved, weighted base. When gently pushed, they will rock back and forth but never fall over.

Legend has it that Daruma was the saintly man who founded Zen Buddhism. One day, after wrapping himself in a robe as protection against the elements, he sat down to meditate. For nine long years, he sat. Unable to walk at the end of that time, he rolled from place to place.

As with many folk toys, there is a superstition connected with owning a Daruma. Sometimes it is made without eyes. The owner, then, is entitled to two wishes. When the first one comes true, one eye is painted on the face. When the second is fulfilled, the other eye is added.

Supplies: A plastic egg shape (any size will do but it must be the type that opens into two halves); Plaster of Paris, enough to fill the bottom half of the egg twice (you will mix two parts of plaster to one part water); acrylic or model enamel paint (select three colors: red, flesh, and brown or black; traditionally, the robe is red); water at room temperature.

Tools: A small plastic throw-away bowl and plastic spoon.

How to make
1. Using a pencil, sketch a face on the top half of the egg. Sketch mittened hands on the bottom half. See Fig. 5-A.
2. Separate egg halves to make them easier to paint. Fill in face and hands with flesh-colored paint. Allow it to dry. Paint the remainder of the egg red and let it dry. Then, using brown or black paint, outline the face, arms, and hands.
3. Paint on the features. Remember, no eyes if you are making a wishing Daruma!
4. Fill the bottom half of the egg almost full of water. Pour the water into the plastic bowl. Dry the egg thoroughly.
5. Using the egg half once more, put two measures of plaster into the water. Let it soak for a minute, then stir until it is the consistency of cream. (Always add plaster to water. It is easier to mix.)
6. Pour the mixture into the bottom half of the egg, Fig. 5-B. It will take several hours to harden. If a little water should stand on top of the plaster, soak it up with a paper towel. Wipe off splashes of plaster immediately!
7. Put the egg halves together and give the Daruma a gentle push. It will rock for you.
8. In time, the plaster will shrink causing it to slide around inside the Daruma. To remedy this, remove the plaster, paint the bottom with gesso or enamel. After the paint dries, pour a little white glue in the bottom of the toy. Then, replace the plaster. Allow the glue to set up for several hours; then put the toy back together.

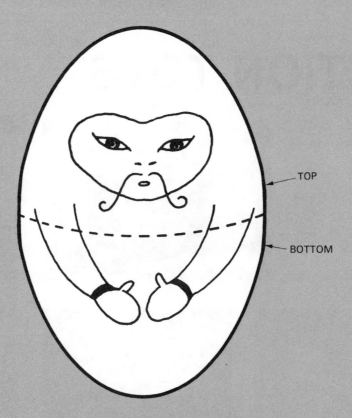

Fig. 5-A. Sketching Daruma features.

TOP

BOTTOM

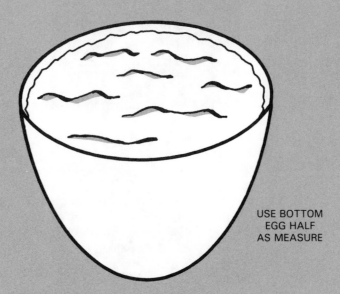

USE BOTTOM
EGG HALF
AS MEASURE

Fig. 5-B. Filling lower half of Daruma with plaster.

ACTION TOYS

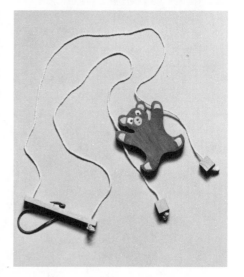

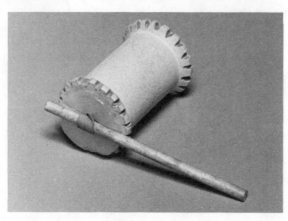

Flap Jack

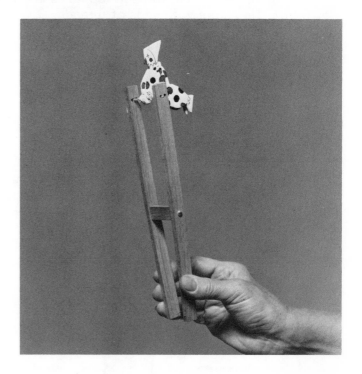

When the Dutch settled in New York, they brought with them the tradition of the "fairings." A fairing was an amusing toy or trinket purchased at one of the great fairs of the Old World.

From the 12th through the 18th century, these huge three-day fairs were sponsored by churches to celebrate a local saint's feast day. These were a major source of entertainment for the populace. The county fairs of today are their offspring.

The Flap Jack is a typical fairing. Because the movements of the figure are created by the force of the twisted string, it is classified as a torsion toy.

Since early toy makers dealt in realism, rather than fantasy, figures used for toys represented familiar people. Our "Jack" is a white-faced clown wearing the costume favored by clowns in early American circuses. The suit is white with large red and black polka dots.

Supplies: Piece of hardwood, 1/2" x 19 1/2" x 1/4" (stock size available in craft and model-making shops); balsa wood, 6" x 3" x 1/8"; two 1/2 in. round head wood screws; 14 in. length of heavy duty carpet and button thread; 4 in. length telephone wire or 16 gauge wire; acrylic gesso; acrylic or model enamel paints—red, white, and black; laundry marking pen; small piece of fine sandpaper; tracing paper.

Tools: Drill and 1/8 in. (or smaller) bit; screwdriver; small saw; craft knife; paint brush; pointed tool, such as an ice pick, to make holes; needle to use with carpet thread; No. 2 pencil.

How to make
1. Trace outlines of patterns in Fig. 6-A with a No. 2 pencil. Interior lines will be added freehand in Step 5.
2. Transfer tracing to the balsa wood. Lay tracing, face down, on the balsa and retrace.
3. Using a craft knife, cut out clown parts. Score the lines first with the knife tip. Then cut away the excess.
4. Sand cut edges lightly. Paint all sides and edges with gesso and allow pieces to dry.
5. Paint the clown. Face, hat, hands, and shoes are white. The suit is white with red and black dots. When dry, add facial features and other details with a marking pen. Refer again to Fig. 6-A.
6. Cut wire into four 1 in. pieces. Make small, flat coils at one end of each wire.
7. Attach the arms. Put the wire through an arm, the body and the other arm. Form a coil with the left-over wire to hold parts together.
8. Attach legs using the same method.
9. Saw hardwood stock into three pieces, (two 9 in. and the third 1 in. long). Mark the 9 in. pieces for holes as shown in Fig. 6-B.
10. Drill thread holes and hole for screws in 9 in. strips.
11. Assemble framework as shown in Fig. 6-C. The 1 in. piece of hardwood is the crossbar for the frame. Use wood screws to hold it in place.
12. Attach clown to framework using needle and doubled thread. Lay the framework flat on the table. Put the clown's arms over its head. Line up thread holes in the hands and frame, Fig. 6-D.

13. Start stringing at the lower hole in one side of the frame. Use the following threading sequence: Thread goes through frame hole, hole in hands, hole in other side of frame. Then return through the top hole in frame, through top holes in hands, and finally, through top hole in other side of frame. Tie a knot with ends of threads.

To make Jack do tricks, hold the bottom ends of the frame in one hand. Gently, squeeze and release the sticks. Occasionally, the clown may have to be turned head over heels a few times to twist the string.

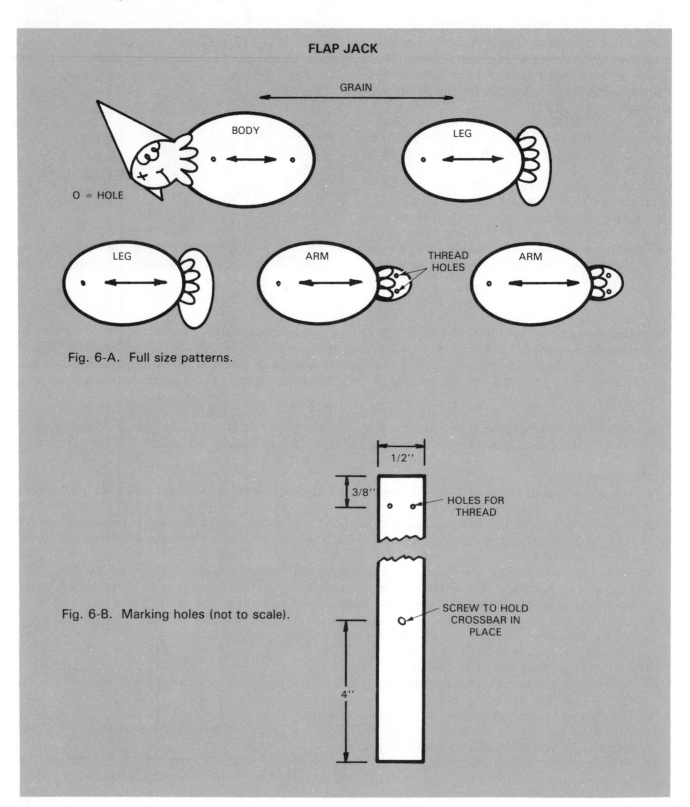

FLAP JACK

GRAIN

BODY

LEG

O = HOLE

LEG

ARM

THREAD HOLES

ARM

Fig. 6-A. Full size patterns.

1/2''

3/8''

HOLES FOR THREAD

Fig. 6-B. Marking holes (not to scale).

SCREW TO HOLD CROSSBAR IN PLACE

4''

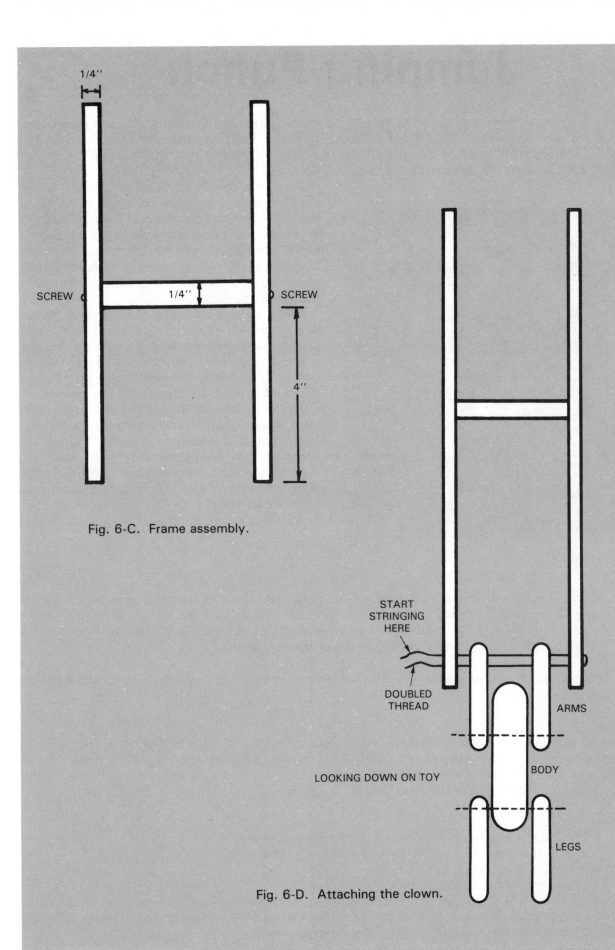

1/4''

SCREW

1/4''

SCREW

4''

Fig. 6-C. Frame assembly.

START
STRINGING
HERE

DOUBLED
THREAD

ARMS

LOOKING DOWN ON TOY

BODY

LEGS

Fig. 6-D. Attaching the clown.

Jumping Punch

To be banned from France was the fate of the pantins. There were doll-like figures made of paper. Jointed arms and legs gyrated when a string was pulled. The advent of machine-made paper and lithography made paper toys possible. The five parts of the toy were printed on heavy paper to be cut out and strung at home.

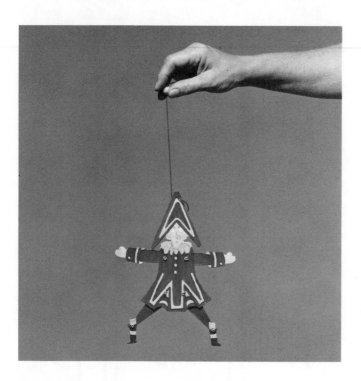

Since the pantin was one of the first paper toys, it was a popular novelty. In 1746 it became a favorite plaything of French children. A year later, it became the darling of the aristocrats. The adult version appeared in many shapes. There were harlequins, columbines, shepherds, ballet dancers—even caricatures of prominent persons.

For a decade the fad spread until nearly everyone was playing with pantins. At this point, the police became concerned for the welfare of women. They tried to banish the toy declaring that women were in danger of bearing children with twisted limbs like pantins.

The craze spread across the Atlantic ocean with similar results. The toys prevailed, however, but did undergo a name change. In America, they are called "Jumping Jack."

At first, they were made from wood. These were followed by designs printed on paper that were to be pasted on wood. Finally, printed paper attached to cardboard was used.

Supplies: Heavy cardboard or mat board, 8'' x 9'', in a light color; telephone wire or 18 gauge covered wire, 12 in. long (it is called stem wire in craft shops); 3 ft. of red string; laundry marking pen; acrylic gesso; white, red, yellow, blue model enamel or acrylic paints (traditionally, Punch has a red coat trimmed with yellow); No. 2 pencil; sheet of tracing paper.

Tools: Sharp craft knife; paintbrushes; ice pick, awl, or other tool with a sharp point to make holes; needle to thread string.

Preparation
1. Trace patterns onto tracing paper with No. 2 pencil. Be sure to trace all the details.
2. Lay tracing paper over the cardboard face down. Retrace outlines and Os and Xs only.
3. Using a knife, cut out all pieces.
4. Make holes as indicated at all Xs and Os.

Assembling
1. Paint both sides of all pieces with gesso. Allow pieces to dry.
2. Place tracings face down on proper pieces and trace off details.
3. Paint all parts on both sides. Let them dry.
4. Use a laundry marking pen to outline details.
5. Cut wire into six 1 1/2 in. pieces. Make a small, tight, flattened coil in one end of each wire.
6. Fasten arms to body, Fig. 7-A, with wire at Xs. Make a coil on the other end of the wire to hold it in place. Do not fasten too tightly; they should move freely.
7. Fasten lower leg, Fig. 7-B, and foot, Fig. 7-C, to upper legs with wire.
8. Fasten the entire leg to the body.

9. Link arms by putting a string through "O" holes and tying. The needle will help.
10. Link legs in the same fashion.
11. Use the 14 in. piece of string to link arm strings and leg strings. Tie one end of the string to the middle of arm string. Repeat with the leg string. Leave the remainder of the long string hang down as a pull cord.
12. Put a 4 in. string through the hole in the hat. Tie it to form a hanging loop.
13. Test action by holding the hanging loop and pulling on the pull cord. Limbs should flap to and fro. If they do not, loosen the wires slightly.

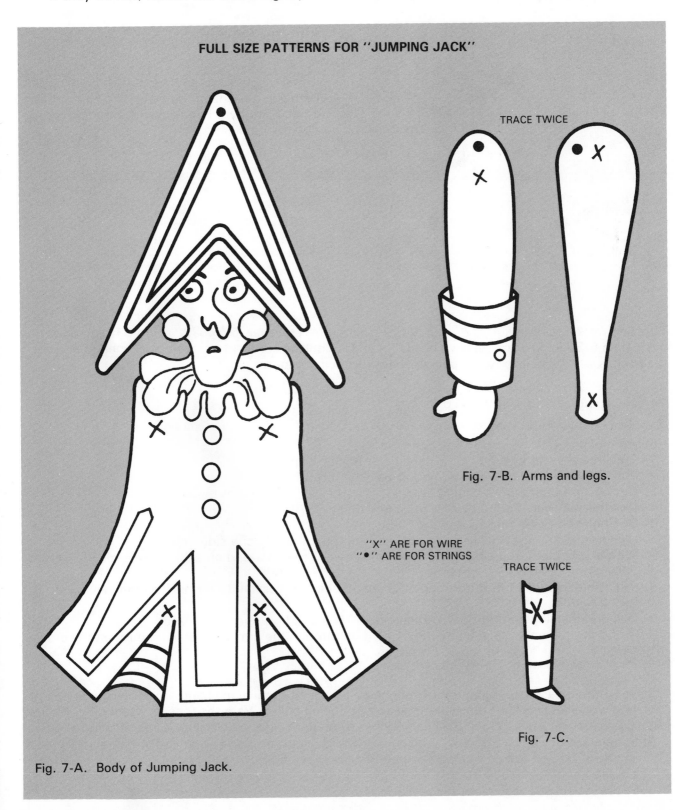

FULL SIZE PATTERNS FOR "JUMPING JACK"

TRACE TWICE

Fig. 7-B. Arms and legs.

"X" ARE FOR WIRE
"●" ARE FOR STRINGS

TRACE TWICE

Fig. 7-C.

Fig. 7-A. Body of Jumping Jack.

Climbing Bear

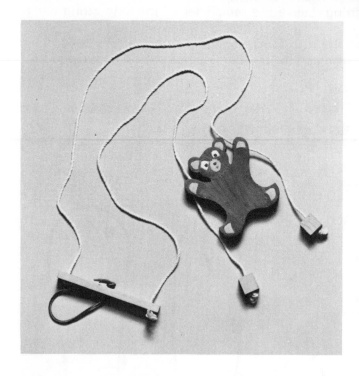

The beginnings of this toy are unknown. Perhaps, it is one of the early wooden toys lovingly made by a Pennsylvania woodcarver.

Supplies: Wood for body, 4 1/2'' x 5'' x 3/4''; wood for crossbar, 5'' x 1/2''; cord 8 ft. long and no more than 5/32 in. in diameter; two beads for ends of pulling cords; permanent black marker or paint; brown paste shoe polish; No. 2 pencil; sheet of tracing paper.

Tools: Coping saw; drill with 3/16 in. bit.

How to make
1. Trace bear pattern using No. 2 pencil and tracing paper.
2. Put the tracing, face down, on wood block and retrace.
3. Cut out the bear with a coping saw.
4. Drill holes in the bear's paws as indicated in Fig. 8-A.
5. Drill holes in the crossbar. See Fig. 8-B.
6. Using a marker or paint, draw in the face and paw details, one side only.
7. With a soft cloth, rub shoe polish over all sides of the bear and crossbar. Use a clean cloth to wipe off excess.
8. Cut 7 in. piece of cord. Put through the center hole on crossbar to form a hanging loop. See Fig. 8-C.
9. Divide remaining cord into two equal parts. Tie a bead on one end of each.
10. String the toy one side at a time. Push cord up through the arm hole, then up through the crossbar. Tie a large knot on top of crossbar.

To make the bear climb, hang the toy on a hook. Take a bead in each hand. Pull down on one cord at a time while keeping light tension on the side not being pulled. Vary the tension alternately. Hands should be close together. When the bear reaches the top, release the tension. It will slide back to the bottom again.

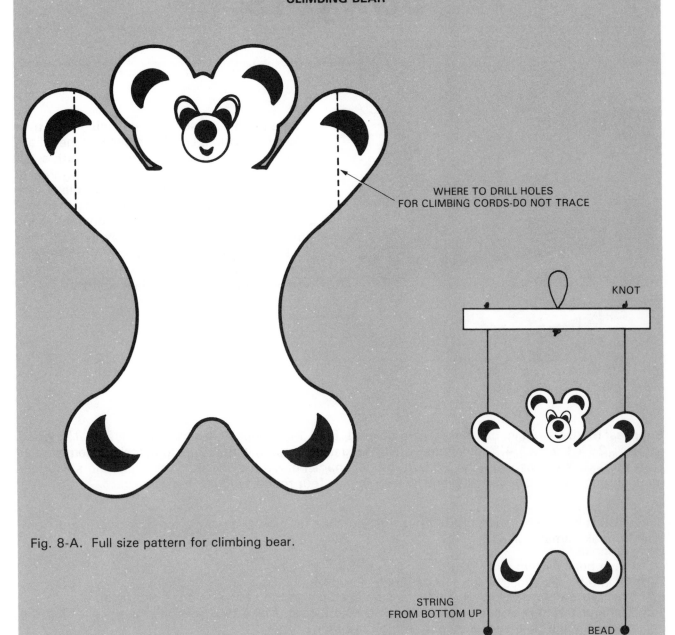

WHERE TO DRILL HOLES
FOR CLIMBING CORDS-DO NOT TRACE

Fig. 8-A. Full size pattern for climbing bear.

KNOT

STRING
FROM BOTTOM UP

BEAD

Fig. 8-C. Stringing the bear (not to scale).

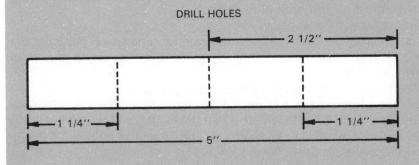

DRILL HOLES

2 1/2''

1 1/4''

1 1/4''

5''

Fig. 8-B. Locating holes in crossbar (not to scale).

Sawyers

When Ben Johnson was describing the toys offered for sale at London's Bartholomew Fair, he mentioned ''the device of the Smith's,'' a push-pull wooden toy on which two figures, in turn, beat on an anvil as the handles were alternately pushed and pulled.

The same type of toy was built by early American boys who whittled away with their jackknives. Because they were more familiar with woodcutters, figures using crosscut saws were more popular than blacksmiths.

Supplies: Medium weight cardboard, light colored, 5'' x 11''; piece of basswood, 7 1/2'' x 1''; wood scrap, 1/2'' x 1/2'' x 1/4''; telephone wire or 18 gauge covered wire, 12 in. long (called stem wire at craft stores); No. 2 pencil; acrylic gesso; model enamel or acrylic paints in assorted colors; laundry marking pen; white glue; small piece of wax paper; four round wooden toothpicks.

Tools: Craft knife; six spring clip clothespins; brushes for glue and paints; ice pick or drawing compass to make small holes.

How to make

1. Trace all patterns in Fig. 9-A (but not the shading on the sawyers' arms and legs).
2. Transfer tracings of sawyer figures to the cardboard. Make two sets. (Remember to flop the tracings each time so traced pattern will transfer.)
3. Transfer patterns of saw and pull strips to basswood.
4. Using craft knife, cut out all parts.
5. Make holes in parts where indicated.
6. Glue sawyers together except in shaded areas indicated on pattern. Separate these areas with wax paper. Clamp joined parts with clothespins until glue dries.
7. Paint edges and both sides of all pieces with gesso. Let dry.
8. Paint sawyers, saw, and pull strips in your choice of colors. Use marking pen to outline details.
9. Cut two 1/16'' deep notches in both sides of a wood scrap. See Fig. 9-B. The scrap should be about 1/4'' thick and about 1/2 in. square.
10. Cut wire into six 2 in. pieces. Make a small flat coil in one end of each piece.
11. To assemble, remove wax paper separating hands and legs. Slide handles of the saw between sawyer's hands. Line up holes using the tip of a toothpick. Leave the toothpick in place until replaced by wires. Do one at a time. After wire is in place, coil the other end to hold it. Wire legs onto pull sticks in the same way. Legs should straddle the sticks.
12. Mark the midpoint between holes in the top stick. Apply a small amount of glue to one groove of

the wood scrap cut in Step 9. Mount it atop the stick at midpoint. Press the edge of the stick into the groove. Let it dry.

13. To make the sawyers work, hold end of top stick in left hand and the end of the bottom stick in the right hand. Gently, push and pull. The sawyers will rock back and forth in a sawing motion.

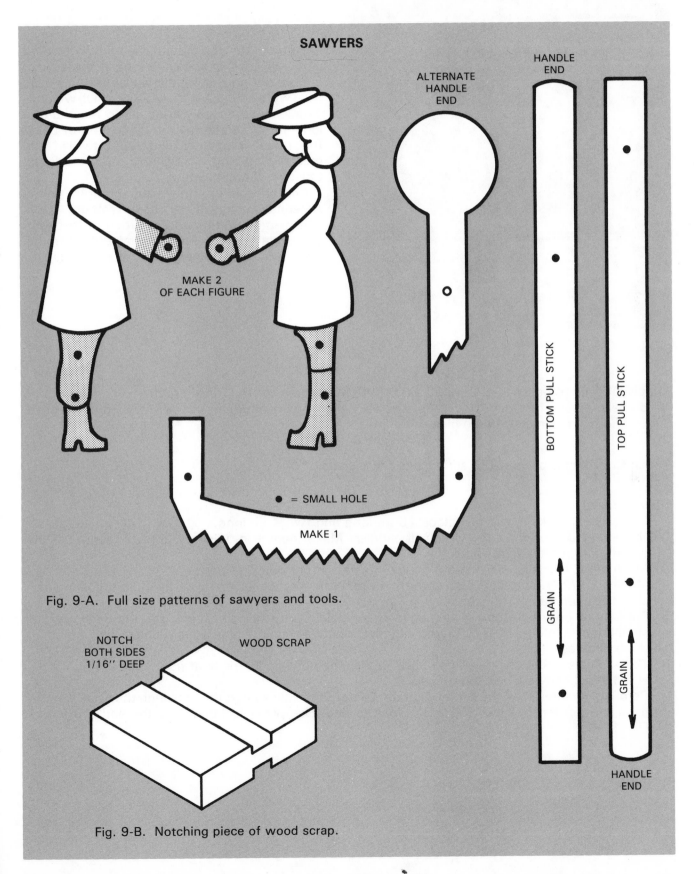

SAWYERS

ALTERNATE HANDLE END

HANDLE END

MAKE 2 OF EACH FIGURE

● = SMALL HOLE

MAKE 1

BOTTOM PULL STICK

TOP PULL STICK

GRAIN

GRAIN

HANDLE END

Fig. 9-A. Full size patterns of sawyers and tools.

NOTCH BOTH SIDES 1/16'' DEEP

WOOD SCRAP

Fig. 9-B. Notching piece of wood scrap.

Pinwheels

To trace the pedigree of the brightly colored pinwheel toys of today, we must go back to Europe during the Middle Ages. In those days they were called windmills. Two small windmill paddles were loosely attached to the end of a long stick. They have the distinction of being the most frequently illustrated toy of the medieval period, appearing on woodcuts, tapestries, and paintings.

Centuries later, they were brought to the American colonies by early settlers. Until 1882, they were made of wood in the traditional way. For a short time after that, metal was used; then paper. Now, plastic is usually substituted.

Supplies: Piece of basswood, 2'' x 5'' x 1/16''; two balloon sticks (These are the bamboo sticks to which balloons are fastened. Novelty stores have them.); steel straight pin with a bead head; bead about 1/2 in. in diameter; white glue.

Tools: Craft knife; pliers; eight spring clip clothespins.

How to make
1. Cut balloon sticks. Make one piece 15 in. long and two 7 in. long.
2. Use a craft knife to cut four windmill paddles. Make them 1 in. wide by 2 1/2 in. long. Let the wood grain run the long way.
3. Make a 1/2 in. deep notch in the middle of the 7 in. sticks.
4. Make a 2 1/2 in. long slit in both ends of sticks. With notches facing up or down, the slit should be about 30 degrees off horizontal. See Fig. 10-A.
5. Put glue on both sides of one long edge of a paddle. Carefully insert it into slit. Mounted paddles should look like Fig. 10-B-1. Clamp with two clothespins until glue dries. Repeat with the other three paddles.
6. To assemble, cross sticks with paddles so that the notches interlock at right angles. Apply glue. Fig. 10-B-2 shows wheel assembled.
7. Before glue dries, stick the pin through the center of the assembly, then through the bead. Finally, push the pin through the long stick close to end. Use pliers to bend over the end of the pin, Fig. 10-C.

PINWHEEL

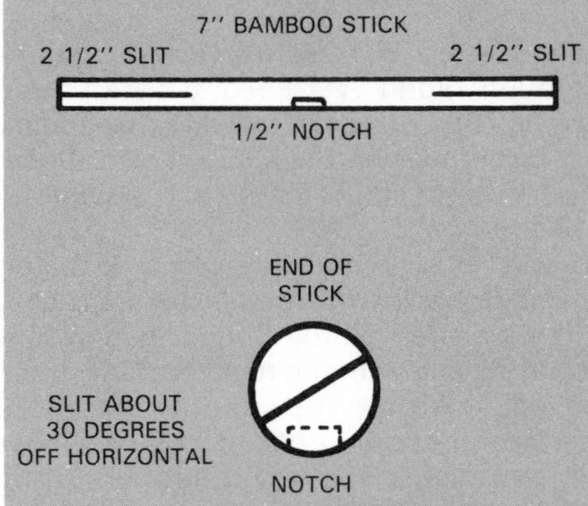

7'' BAMBOO STICK
2 1/2'' SLIT
2 1/2'' SLIT
1/2'' NOTCH
END OF STICK
SLIT ABOUT 30 DEGREES OFF HORIZONTAL
NOTCH

Fig. 10-A. Notching and slitting bamboo (not to scale).

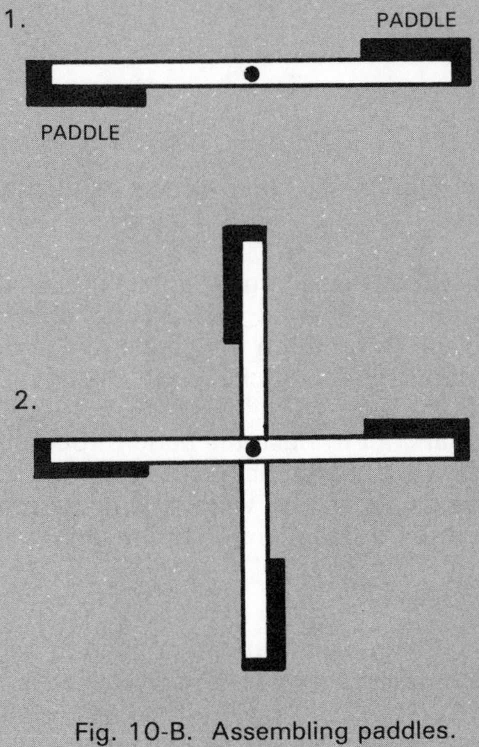

1.
PADDLE
PADDLE
2.

Fig. 10-B. Assembling paddles.

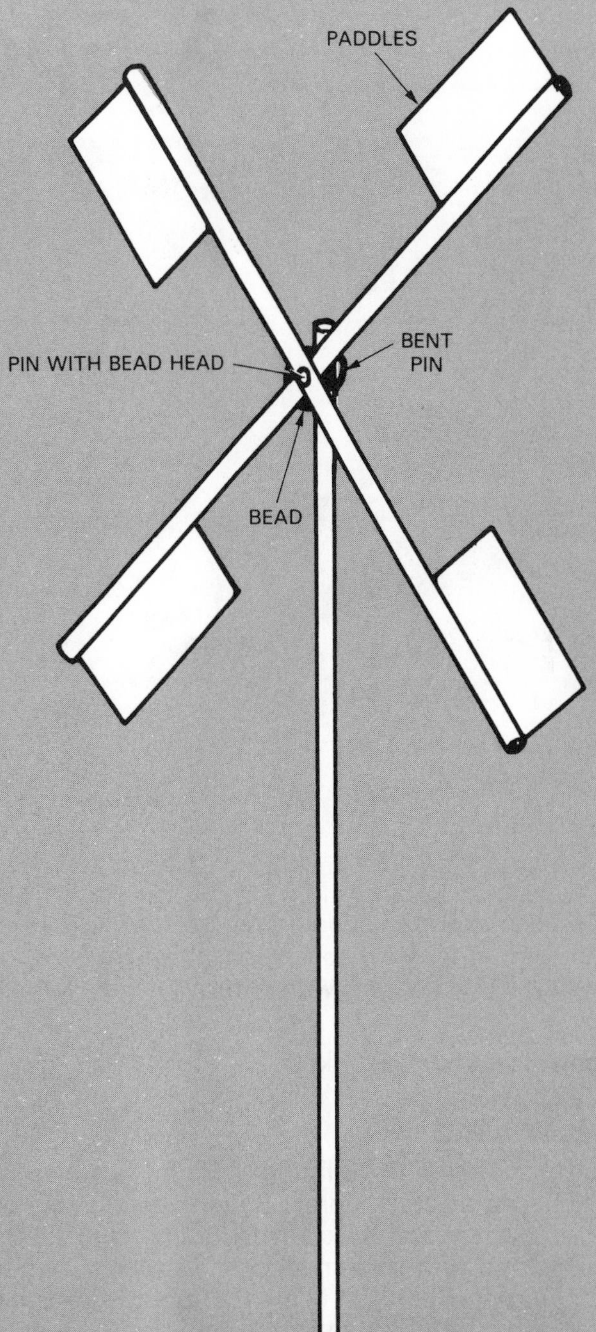

PADDLES
PIN WITH BEAD HEAD
BENT PIN
BEAD

Fig. 10-C. Assembled wheel.

Grandpa Bill's Tank, A Spool Toy

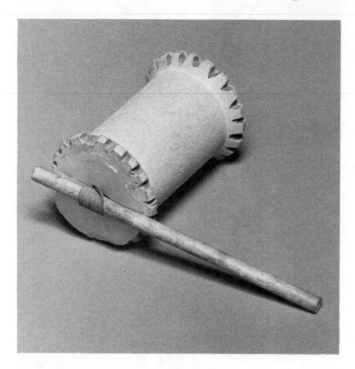

When Grandpa Bill was a boy, our country was fighting World War I. Toys were scarce because toy factories were making weapons. In fact, some men on the Council of National Defense thought that Christmas should be abolished.

A group of toy manufacturers appeared before the Council with samples of their best toys. The members of the Council had such a good time playing with the toys that Christmas was saved.

Children of those days had to make the most of their playthings. They used odds and ends from their homes. The tank was one of the motion toys they built.

Supplies: Wooden spool, any size; two 1/2 in. nails or brads; rubber band; dowel, 1/8 in. diameter and 4 in. long; inch square chunk of paraffin; small metal container for holding hot paraffin; larger container for heating water; throw-away foil pie tin.

Tools: Hammer; craft knife.

How to make
1. Cut notches in both ridges of the spool at 1/4 in. intervals, Fig. 11-A. Wood spools can be purchased at craft stores. (Plastic spools can be notched with a file or a very hot ice pick.) Use of styrofoam spools is not recommended.
2. Melt paraffin in a small can. Set can in larger container of water. Place larger container over the fire. After paraffin is melted, pour it into the pie tin. When it is cool enough to handle, shape a washer nearly the same diameter as the spool. Make a hole in it to match the hole in the spool.
3. Hammer two small nails into one end of the spool leaving about 1/4 in. sticking out, as shown in Fig. 11-A.
4. To assemble the tank, loop the rubber band over the nail to anchor it. Push the band through the spool and through the paraffin washer. Put one end of the dowel through the open loop of the rubber band alongside the washer, Fig. 11-B. The dowel serves as a crank for winding up the rubber band. When the spool is placed on a flat surface it also prevents the rubber band from unwinding too rapidly.

To make the tank move, hold the spool in one hand. Crank the dowel with the other hand to wind up the band. Place the tank on the floor or table top with the end of the dowel resting on the surface. Let it run.

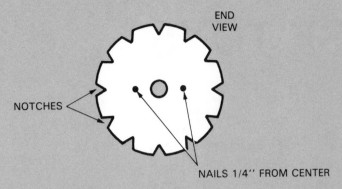

END
VIEW

NOTCHES

NAILS 1/4'' FROM CENTER

Fig. 11-A. Preparing the spool.

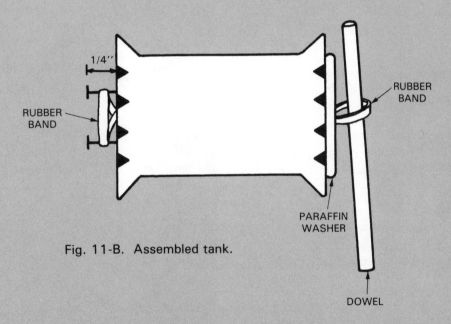

1/4''

RUBBER
BAND

RUBBER
BAND

PARAFFIN
WASHER

Fig. 11-B. Assembled tank.

DOWEL

NOISE TOYS

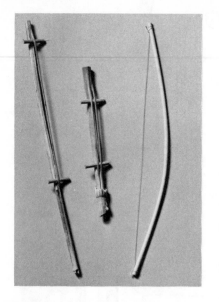

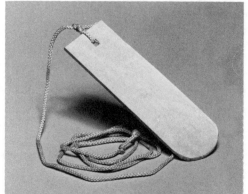

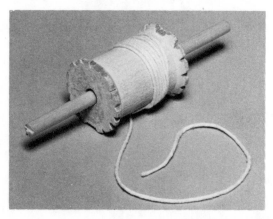

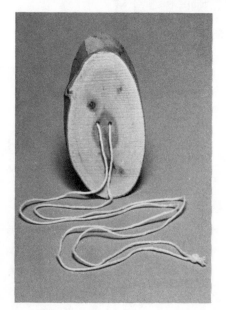

Spool Tick Tacks

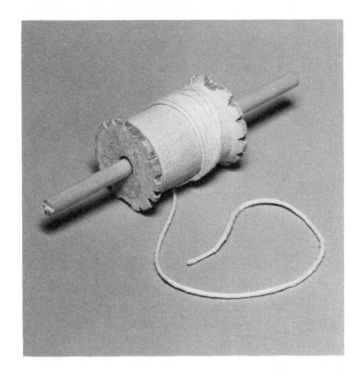

In the last half of the 19th century, there was a large-scale Irish immigration to the United States. They brought with them the Halloween customs. Part of the fun was playing pranks on the neighbors. The raucous sound of a spool tick tack on a windowpane was known to startle many a householder.

Supplies: Wooden or plastic thread spool—any size; stick, 8" x 1/8" diameter; piece of strong cord about 3 ft. long.

Tools: Craft knife.

How to make
1. With the craft knife cut notches in the edges of both ends of the spool, Fig. 12-A. Use a file to notch plastic spools.
2. Wind the string tightly around the spool. Leave one end hang down. Put the 8 in. long stick through the center of the spool. Fig. 12-B.

To work the tick tack, wind the string around the spool and hold the end of the stick with your left hand. Place the spool against a window. Pull the string with your right hand.

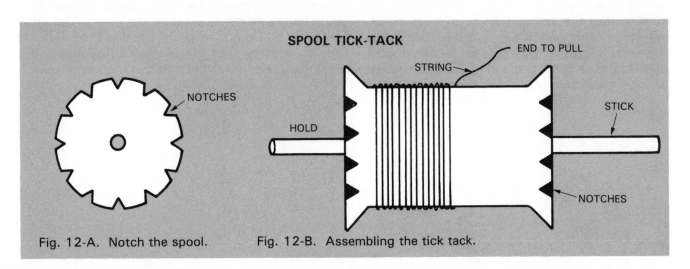

SPOOL TICK-TACK

NOTCHES

END TO PULL

STRING

HOLD

STICK

NOTCHES

Fig. 12-A. Notch the spool.   Fig. 12-B. Assembling the tick tack.

Buzz Saw

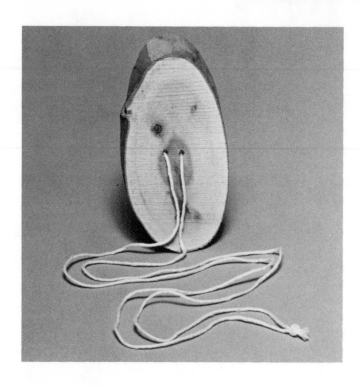

Toys that make noise have fascinated children the world over in any age. The buzz saw is such a toy. It produces a buzzing sound similar to that made by a saw. Variations of the toy have been found by archeologists excavating ancient civilizations.

Children of British soldiers quartered in colonial America played with such toys. A camp dating from 1781 was excavated in 1921. It yielded several coins that had been made into buzz saws.

Lacking coins, children made the disk out of any suitable material. Popular substitutes were fashioned from wood chips. A button, if available, was even better; the holes were already there.

Supplies: Strong cord, length about 40 in.; wood chip, buttom, play coin or any disk-shaped object from 1 to 3 in. diameter through which holes can be drilled.

Tools: Scissors; drill or other tool for making holes.

How to make

1. If the disk does not already have holes, find the center and mark it. Drill two holes equally distant from the center. They should be about 1/2 in. apart, Fig. 13-A.
2. Put the cord through both holes and tie the ends in a knot, Fig. 13-B.

To work the buzz saw, hold a loop of the cord in either hand with the disk midway between. With hands close together, swing the disk around and around several times to twist the string. Tension the cord to start the disk spinning. Then alternately tighten and relax the tension on the string. The disk will spin first in one direction and then in the other, Fig. 13-C. Do not relax the tension too much or too fast. Keep tension light and let the shortening and lengthening of the twisted string guide the hands. The disk will respond with a buzzing sound that rises and falls in pitch according to the speed at which it is spinning.

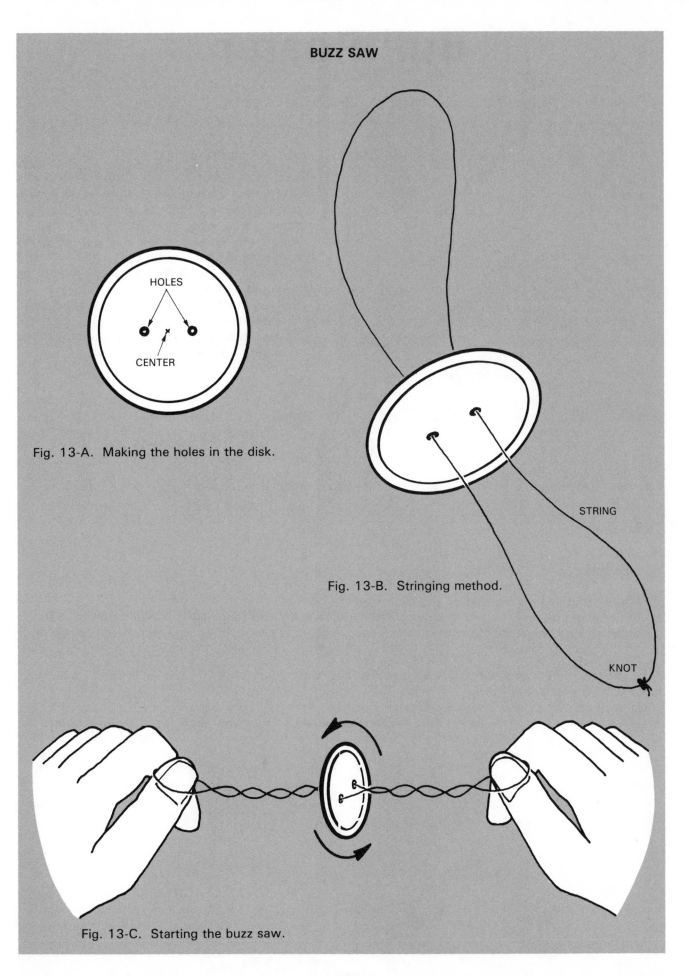

Fig. 13-A. Making the holes in the disk.

Fig. 13-B. Stringing method.

Fig. 13-C. Starting the buzz saw.

Bull Roarer

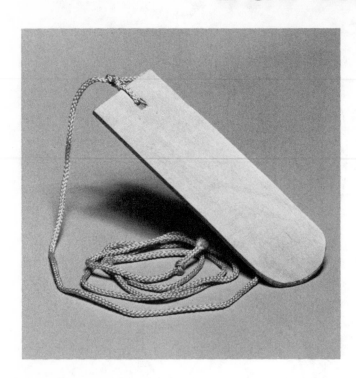

The throaty fluttering sound of the "bull roarer" has been heard for centuries by many civilizations. Sometimes it was used in religious ceremonies; sometimes as an aid to herding cattle; and sometimes just for fun.

American Indians used them in religious ceremonies in times of drought. They thought that when rain heard the sound of thunder the rain would come.

Bull roarers has such appeal for pioneer boys that they made their own.

Today, in some areas of the United States, bull roarers are used to drive hogs.

Supplies: Basswood, 8'' x 2 1/2'' x 3/16''; polycord, chalk line, or strong fish line 40 in. long.

Tools: Craft knife.

How to make
1. Trace the pattern and transfer it to basswood. Cut out the bull roarer.
2. Make the hole as indicated on the pattern, Fig. 14-A.
3. Put one end of cord through the hole. Tie with a bowline knot, Fig. 14-B. Since rope ends tend to ravel, put a knot in the other end of the cord. You may prefer to whip it to prevent unraveling.

To use the roarer, let it hang straight down so the cord can untwist. Then whirl it rapidly over your head to hear the bull roar.

Be very careful to stay away from other children. This can be a dangerous toy. Check the cord often to be sure it is not wearing out. Prepare for wet weather; you might start a cloud burst!

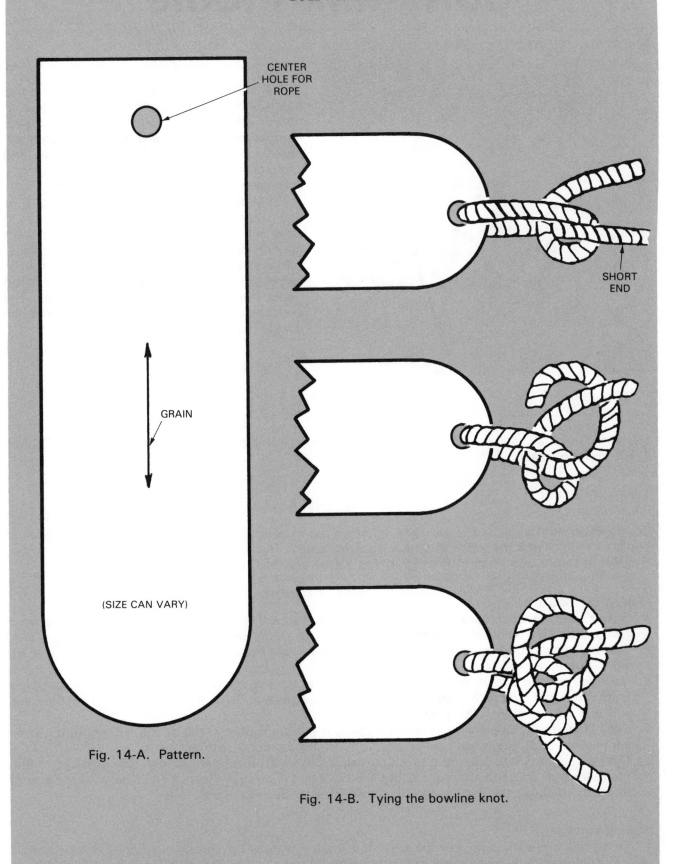

CENTER
HOLE FOR
ROPE

GRAIN

(SIZE CAN VARY)

SHORT
END

Fig. 14-A. Pattern.

Fig. 14-B. Tying the bowline knot.

Cornstalk Fiddle

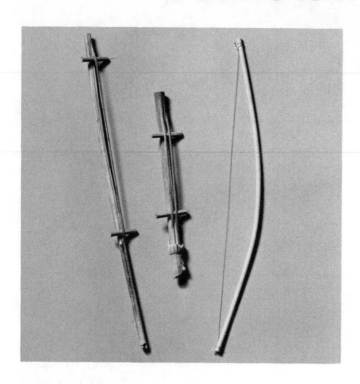

The making of fiddles from cornstalks has been handed down as a folk craft from generation to generation. Since corn was first grown in America, this musical instrument is uniquely American. It is questionable whether the scraping sound produced was music; still, it was sweet to the ears of the maker!

Traditionally, the materials came out of rustic surroundings. Thus, it will not be hard in smaller town and rural communities to collect the necessary materials at little or no expense.

Many gardens will yield dried stalks from sweetcorn and sticks can often be collected under trees in residential neighborhoods. The craftperson's scrap box will also contain usable materials.

Supplies: Cornstalk; stick or dowel about 14 in. long for bow; four sticks 1/8 in. diameter and about 1 1/2 in. long; rosin.

Tools: Craft knife.

Cornstalks should be picked in the early fall when the corn is being harvested. Strip off dried leaves. The stalk is thicker at the base than the top and is jointed. There is a groove down one side. This, too, is wider at the bottom than at the top. It will act as a sounding board. See Fig. 15-A.

Making the fiddle
1. Select a section of cornstalk that is near the base. You will need a piece with a full length between joints plus a half length beyond each joint. Cut the stalk off between joints as shown in Fig. 15-A.
2. The stalk has a tough outer covering which is quite rigid when dry. Soak the section in water for 30 minutes.
3. Now you are ready to make the "strings." Turn the stalk so the groove is up. Slip the point of the knife through the ridge formed along one side of the groove. Guide the blade to come out between 1/8 and 1/4 in. from point of entry.
4. Slide blade along lengthwise of the stalk to loosen a narrow strip nearly the full length between joints. Repeat on the other side of groove to make a second "string."
5. Cut two sticks 3/4 to 1 in. long to act as stops. Slice a little material off one side of sticks to flatten them and reduce thickness to about 1/8 in. or less. Carefully insert the sticks under the strings to lift them above the stalk where they can vibrate. See Fig. 15-B.

Making bows
1. To make a cornstalk bow, cut the stalk in the same way as for making the fiddle. Soak the stalk and then use the knife to make only one string. Insert short sticks, as in Step 5, to lift the bow-string away from the stalk. See Fig. 15-C.
2. To make a bow from a dowel or stick cut a small slot in the ends of the stick. Slip one end of the

string into a slot, wrap it around the stick and tie it with two half hitches. With the stick bowed for tension, fasten string to opposite end. See Fig. 15-D.

Rub rosin on the strings. Play the toy like a conventional fiddle.

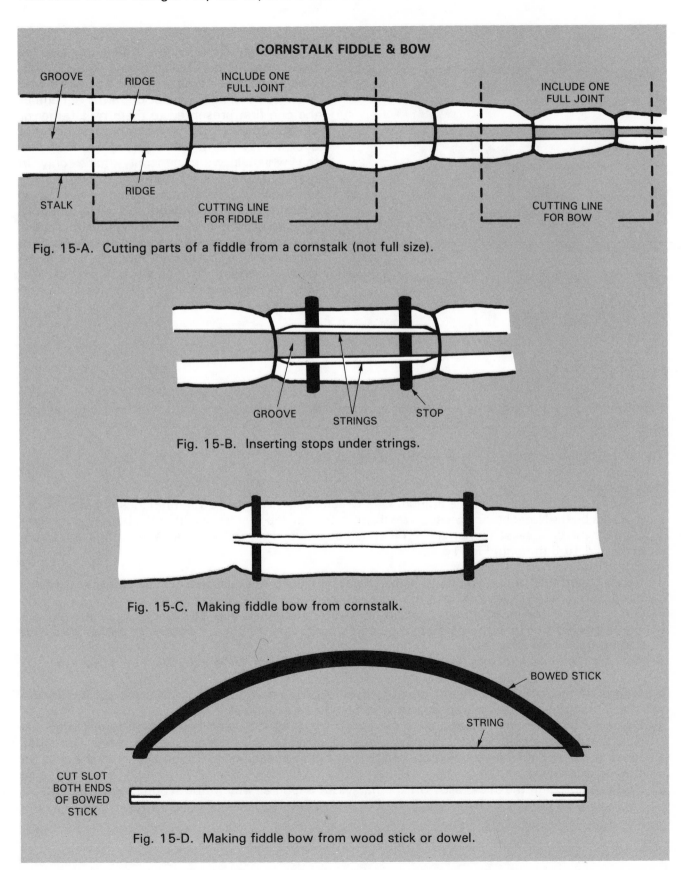

CORNSTALK FIDDLE & BOW

GROOVE
RIDGE
INCLUDE ONE FULL JOINT
INCLUDE ONE FULL JOINT
STALK
RIDGE
CUTTING LINE FOR FIDDLE
CUTTING LINE FOR BOW

Fig. 15-A. Cutting parts of a fiddle from a cornstalk (not full size).

GROOVE   STRINGS   STOP

Fig. 15-B. Inserting stops under strings.

Fig. 15-C. Making fiddle bow from cornstalk.

BOWED STICK
STRING
CUT SLOT BOTH ENDS OF BOWED STICK

Fig. 15-D. Making fiddle bow from wood stick or dowel.

Willow Whistle

The origin of the willow whistle goes so far back into history that no one knows from where it came. Many American children who grew up in small towns or on farms remember the one first presented to them by a father or older brother. If they were to stop and ponder over it they might be surprised to recall that the whistles were generally made only in Spring. There was a reason for this which will be explained in the instructions.

Probably, once having followed the construction of the first whistle, youngsters went on to produce crude copies of their own. The steps are very simple although it is easy to spoil the whistle if you are not careful. The bark is fragile and will split if handled too roughly.

Supplies: Short section of freshly cut branch from a willow tree. It should be as big around as the thumb or about an inch in diameter.

Tools: Jackknife or utility knife; small wood mallet (optional).

How to make
1. Select a smooth section of the branch. One which has no twigs or other branches growing out of it works best. (Note: branch must be freshly cut so that sap is still present in the bark.) Springtime is about the only season when this project can be made easily without damage to the bark. Use a section 4 to 5 in. long, Fig. 16-A.
2. Cut off both ends square.
3. Carefully tap the bark all around to help separate it from the wood. Use a small mallet or the handle of the jackknife, carefully slip the bark off the wood, Fig. 16-B.
4. Cut a notch in the wood about 1 5/8 in. away from one end, Fig. 16-C.
5. Cut a shallow slot from the notch to the nearest end. This will be the airway for the whistle. Slot can be flat or vee shaped.
6. Replace the bark in its original position. Cut away bark over the notch. See Fig. 16-D.

Variations of the whistle. Different construction techniques will produce different pitches in the whistle. There are several variations with which you can experiment:
1. Do not notch the stick. Instead, slide the bark off to produce several holes at different intervals. Space them far enough apart so they can be covered by the fingers. See Fig. 16-E. Cut away most of the wood removed. Replace only a short plug at each end. Cut an airway in the plug for the mouthpiece.
2. Without notching the stick, slide off the bark. Cut a long airway in the wood. Length is variable depending on number of holes you intend to make. See Fig. 16-F. Cut holes in the bark as in the previous instructions. Replace the wood inside the bark.

To play a whistle with variable pitch, place fingers over the holes. Blow into the whistle lifting fingers from holes. Sound will change as you uncover different holes.

WILLOW WHISTLE

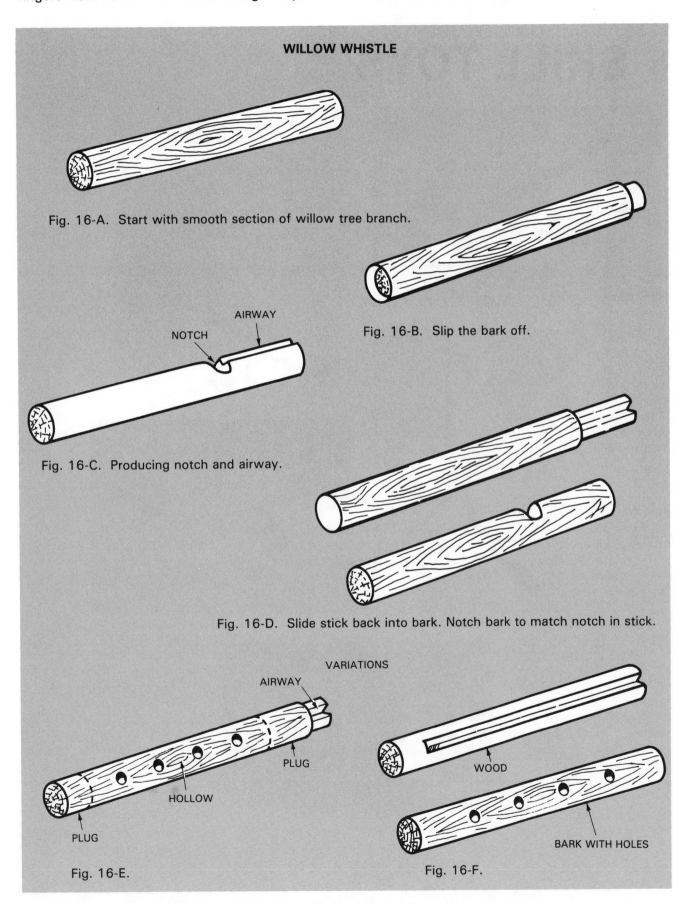

Fig. 16-A. Start with smooth section of willow tree branch.

Fig. 16-B. Slip the bark off.

NOTCH   AIRWAY

Fig. 16-C. Producing notch and airway.

Fig. 16-D. Slide stick back into bark. Notch bark to match notch in stick.

VARIATIONS

AIRWAY

PLUG

HOLLOW

PLUG

Fig. 16-E.

WOOD

BARK WITH HOLES

Fig. 16-F.

SKILL TOYS

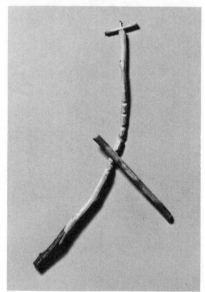

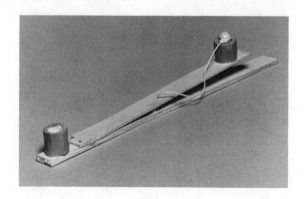

Jacob's Ladder

Intriguing is the adjective that best describes a Jacob's ladder. It is named for the Jacob's Ladder in the Bible (Genesis, 28:12).

Six to eight flat wooden blocks are taped together in such a way that they are double hinged. When the top block is held by the edges and tipped forward to touch the second block, then quickly tipped backwards to touch it again, the second block appears to tumble, end-over-end, down the ladder. As long as the rocking motion is continued, the illusion continues.

Created in Japan, it was imported to the United States and England in the early 1900s. It is considered one of the best toys of the early 20th century.

Supplies: Lattice stripping, 24'' x 2 1/4'' x 1/4'' (basswood or heavy cardboard may be substituted); three yd. of 1/2'' twill tape (one package); scrap cardboard, 2 1/4'' x 3''; wax paper; white glue; sandpaper, small piece.

Tools: Old watercolor brush for applying glue; scissors; pencil; saw.

How to make

1. Saw lattice strip into eight 3 by 2 1/4 in. blocks. Sand sawed edges.
2. Cut 21 strips of twill tape 5 in. long.
3. Cut cardboard template for use as gluing guide, Fig. 17-A.
4. Cut seven pieces of wax paper, the size of the blocks.
5. Begin assembly. Lay a block down on the table. Place the template on top. Lightly trace around all cut out sections. This indicates where to glue tape. Repeat with six more blocks. (Leave one unmarked for the end.)
6. Glue tape onto seven blocks at marked spots. Do not get glue on edges of the blocks. Brush on glue in a thin, even coat. Allow it to dry.
7. Lay one block, tape side down, on the table. All tapes should be extended. See Fig. 17-B.
8. Bring tape ends up and over the block. See Fig. 17-C.
9. Place second block, tape side down, on top of first one. Tapes should be extended, Fig. 17-D.
10. Bring short ends up over the edges of the second block and glue to block. Wipe off any excess glue, Fig. 17-E.
11. Cover block with a piece of wax paper.
12. Bring long tapes up over block, Fig. 17-F. Go back to Step 9 and repeat process until seven blocks are stacked and glued.
13. Place last block on stack. Bring up tapes from seventh block over last block and glue.
14. Allow glue to dry at least four hours. Remove wax paper.

The ladder can be embellished as in the Victorian manner. Slip pieces of brightly colored decorative paper under the tapes. Cut them slightly smaller than the blocks. If preferred, plain twill tape can be replaced with decorative tape. Do not use tape that will stretch.

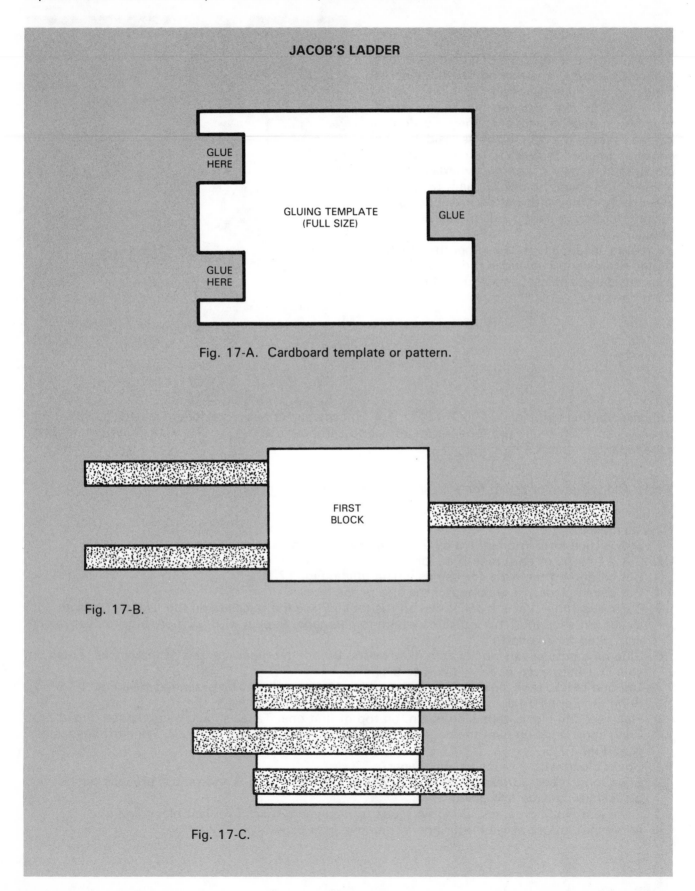

JACOB'S LADDER

GLUE
HERE

GLUE

GLUING TEMPLATE
(FULL SIZE)

GLUE
HERE

Fig. 17-A. Cardboard template or pattern.

FIRST
BLOCK

Fig. 17-B.

Fig. 17-C.

Fig. 17-D.

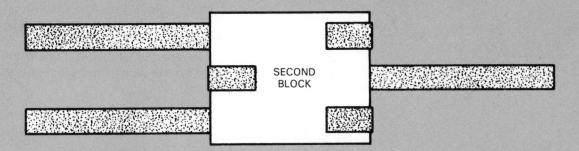

Fig. 17-E.

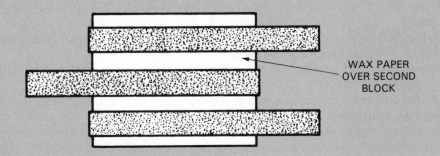

WAX PAPER
OVER SECOND
BLOCK

Fig. 17-F.

Cup and Ball

French aristocrats of the 16th century were a playful lot. They had several favorite toys, the pantin and the bilbocquet. The general public was quick to imitate them and the bilbocquet became the rage.

Travelers returning to England from the Continent introduced it to England. There the name was changed to "Cup and Ball."

The toy then journeyed to America. It became one of the earliest games played by American children.

It is a simple toy, easily made. The ball is attached to the stem and cup with about 25 inches of string. The end of the stem opposite the cup is pointed. The object is to swing the ball so that it goes into the cup or onto the point. The size of the toy varies. The stem may range from 3 to 14 in. long. The ball could be as small as a bead or larger than a golf ball, depending on the size of the stem and the cup.

Supplies: Small dried gourd; eight dried corn husks; two yards, or more, of string; section of cornstalk or a stick 6 to 7 in. long and the thickness of a pencil; white glue; water; pencil; towel.

Tools: Craft knife.

How to make

1. Soak corn husks and string in water.
2. With the pencil, draw a circle around the gourd. This will give a cutting guide for making a cup of the gourd.
3. Soak the gourd in water about 20 minutes to soften its skin. When you can pierce the skin with the tip of a knife, carefully cut on guideline, Fig. 18-A.
4. Remove seeds and membrane. Make a hole in the bottom of the cup big enough to receive the end of the stick, Fig. 18-B.
5. Wrap the wet corn husks in a towel. Using three or four at a time, trim off the hard end and tear husks into strips about 1 in. wide.
6. Begin constructing the ball with a core made from several husks tightly rolled into a tight ball. Continue wrapping husks around the core. When adding a fresh strip of husk, cover the end of the preceding one. Stop when the ball is about 1 1/2 in. in diameter. To hold the ball together, wrap it with string in all directions. Leave a short length of beginning end hang out. Use it to tie off.
7. Now, tie the ball to the end of a 30 in. piece of string. Go around the ball like you would tie a package. This will take about 8 in. of the string. Tie off with a knot. The remainder of the string will be used to attach the ball to the cup.
8. Insert the stick handle into the hole previously made in the bottom of the gourd cup. Apply glue generously inside and outside the hole.
9. Tie the ball to the stick where the stick joins the cup, Fig. 18-C.

To use the ball and cup, hold the cup upright letting the ball hang down. Swing the handle upward to toss the ball into the air. Try to catch the ball in the cup.

CUP AND BALL

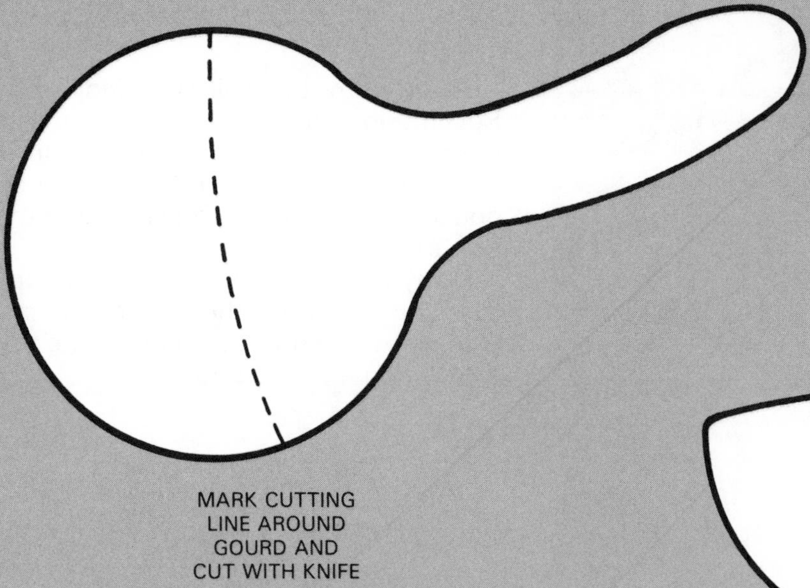

MARK CUTTING
LINE AROUND
GOURD AND
CUT WITH KNIFE

Fig. 18-A.

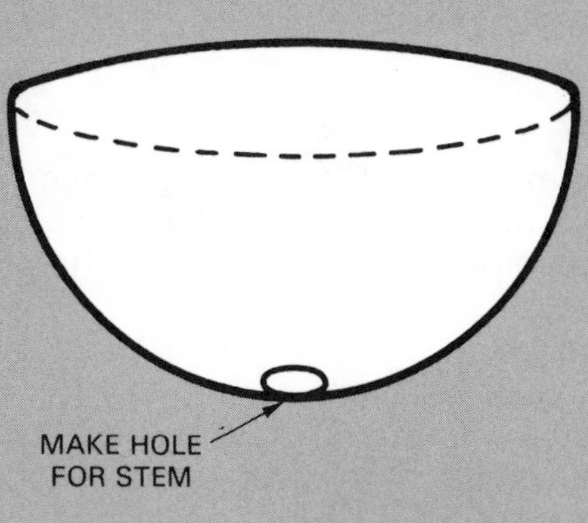

MAKE HOLE
FOR STEM

Fig. 18-B.

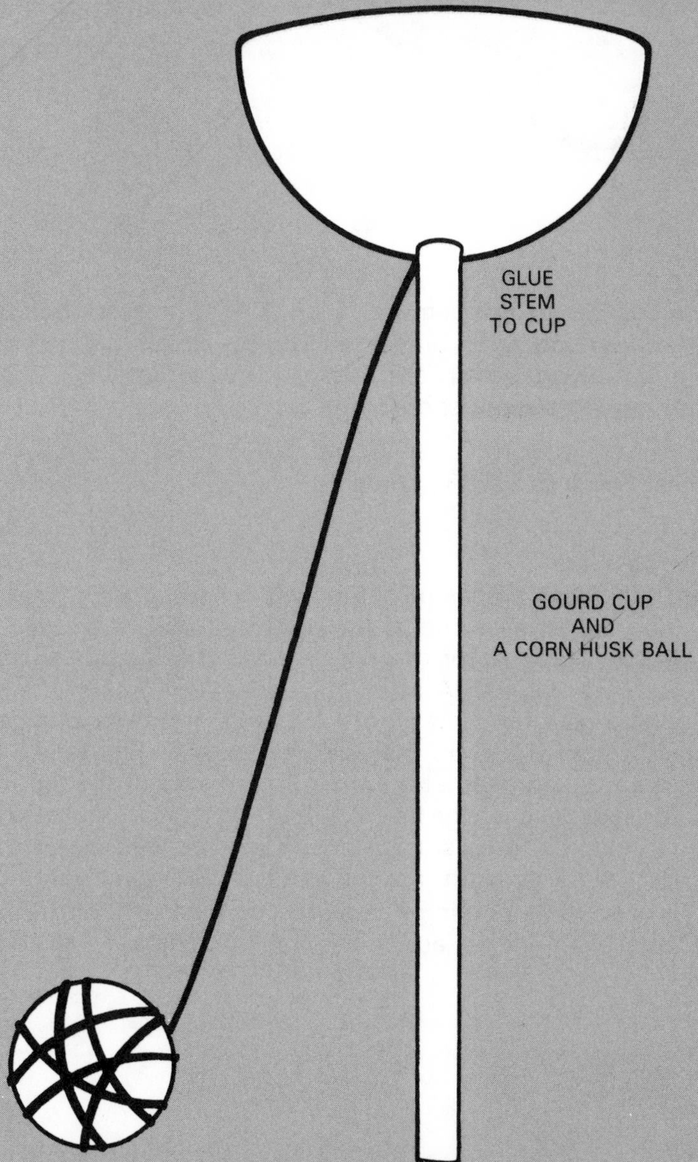

GLUE
STEM
TO CUP

GOURD CUP
AND
A CORN HUSK BALL

Fig. 18-C.

Flipperdinger

From grim beginnings during the French Revolution, this toy has become a "play pretty" of our southern uplands. In France it was known as "Le Pendu," the hangman's noose, an unspoken protest against the wholesale executions.

Many refugees from the Revolution entered the United States through the Port of New Orleans. This could account for the toy finding a new home in the South.

Supplies: Section of bamboo, 9″ x 3/4″ diameter, for blowpipe; cork to plug hole in smaller end; section of bamboo, 1″ x 3/8″ diameter for air tube; bare wire, 18 gage by 18 in. long; lightweight bare wire, 2 in. long; small cork, balsa, or styrofoam ball, 1/2 in. diameter; white glue. (Bamboo is sold in most garden supply shops.)

Tools: Small saw; drill; pliers.

How to make
1. Check both pieces of bamboo for obstructions. You must be able to blow through them.
2. Plug the smaller end of the blowpipe with the cork. Glue it to prevent it from falling out.
3. Make a groove for the wire around the outside of the blowpipe 1/2 in. away from the plugged end. See Fig. 19-A.
4. Drill a hole for the air tube 1 1/4 in. from the plugged end.
5. Fit the air tube into the hole and glue it, Fig. 19-A.
6. Make a 1 in. diameter loop in the middle of the 18 in. section of wire. Wrap the rest of the wire together except the last 2 1/2 in. Wrap this untwisted section around the groove in the end of the blowpipe and twist the ends. Stick the wire ends into the cork, Fig. 19-B.
7. Run the 2 in. wire through the ball. Make a hook in one end. Glue it in place, Fig. 19-C.

To use the flipperdinger, seat the cork ball on top of the air tube with the wire hook upward. Blow into the blowpipe to launch the ball into the air. Try to hook the ball on the hoop.

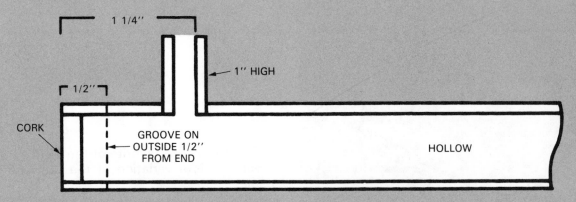

Fig. 19-A. Cross section of blowpipe
(not to scale).

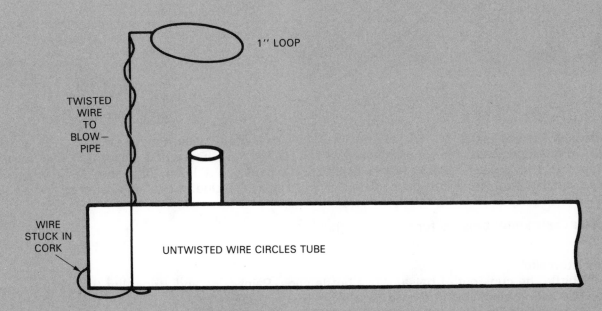

Fig. 19-B. Attaching wirehoop to blowpipe.

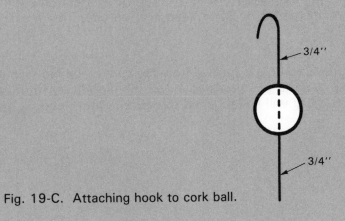

Fig. 19-C. Attaching hook to cork ball.

Flip Ball

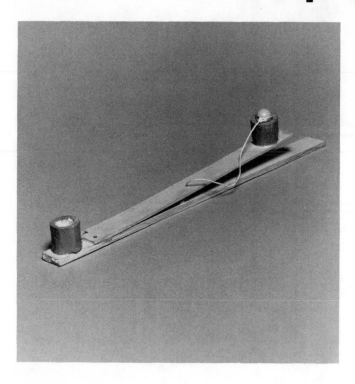

This toy was a favorite of the 16th century French. It is a variation of the Cup and Ball game.

Supplies: For base strip, 11 1/2'' x 3/4'' x 3/16'' basswood piece; for flip stick, 8 1/2'' x 3/4'' x 1/8'' basswood piece; for spring block, 3/4'' x 1/8'' x 1/8'' basswood piece; two 1/4'' nails; for cups, two 1 in. sq. balsa blocks or two plastic bottle caps about 1/2 in. high and 1/2 in. in diameter; bead small enough to fit into cups; string, 8 in. long; white glue; model enamel or acrylic paints.

Tools: Craft knife; brushes for paint and glue.

How to make
1. Whittle the cups out of balsa or use bottle caps. Paint cups and strips. Let them dry.
2. Glue spring block and cup onto base strip. See Fig. 20-A.
3. Drill a hole in the middle of the flip stick 4 1/2 in. from the left end. Glue cup onto stick, Fig. 20-B.
4. Tie a big knot in one end of the string. Put the other end through the hole in the flip stick. Knot should be on the underside, Fig. 20-C.
5. Glue the flip stick onto the base strip 1/4 in. from the cup. Reinforce with nails, Fig. 20-D.
6. Thread the string through the bead. Place bead in base cup. This measures correct length for string. Tie in place.

   To use the flip ball game, try to get the ball from the cup on the flip strip to the cup on the base. Hold the toy in one hand while you press down on the flip stick with thumb of the other hand. When you release it, the ball will be launched toward the other cup.

FLIP BALL

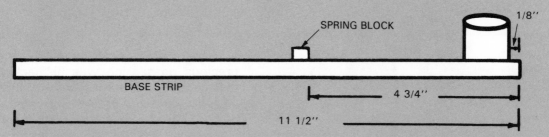

Fig. 20-A. Gluing spring block and cup to base strip.

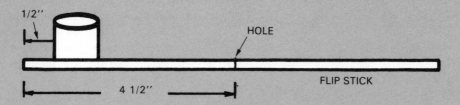

Fig. 20-B. Gluing cup to flip stick.

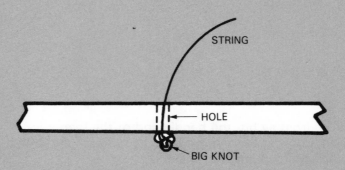

Fig. 20-C. Attaching string to flip stick.

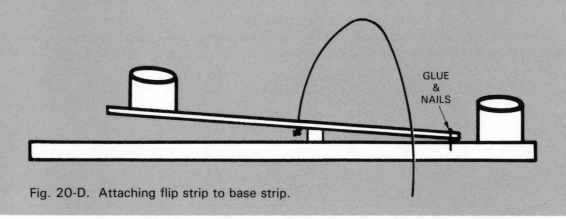

Fig. 20-D. Attaching flip strip to base strip.

Whimmeydiddle

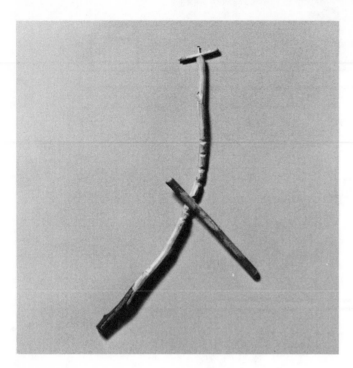

There was a time when a boy's most precious possession was his jackknife. This was especially true for a country boy. His skill with the knife determined the number of toys he had. The knife was also a source of income. He could make things such as brooms that could be sold in town.

A whimmeydiddle is a easy toy for a beginning whittler. It is a notched stick with a rotor loosely nailed to one end. When another stick is rubbed across the notches, the rotor spins. Some folks call it magic. Others say that it is a lie detector. However regarded, it is fun to use.

Possibly, the idea for this toy came to this country from Africa. Missionaries who have served in Africa tell us that similar toys are common there.

Supplies: Stick of green (unseasoned) hardwood 8 to 9 in. long (need not be straight); rubbing stick of same wood, 4 in. long; for rotor, stick of same wood 1 1/2 in. long; for fastening rotor, 1 in. long wire nail (4 penny or smaller).

Tools: Jackknife, small drill and bit.

How to make
1. Whittle away the bark from all but the handle end of the long stick.
2. Cut six or seven wide notches. Start about 5 in. away from handle end. Space them evenly about 1/2 in. apart and keep them in line, Fig. 21-A.
3. Shape the rotor by whittling flats on either side of the middle where the hole will be drilled.
4. Find center of rotor and drill a hole slightly larger than diameter of nail, Fig. 21-B.
5. Drive nail through the hole in the rotor and into the end of the stick. Do not drive the nail too deep; rotor must be able to rotate freely.
6. Using the jackknife, remove some of the bark from the shorter rubbing stick.

To use the whimmydiddle, rub shorter stick briskly back and forth across notches. Rotor will rock back and forth and then spin—if you do it properly.

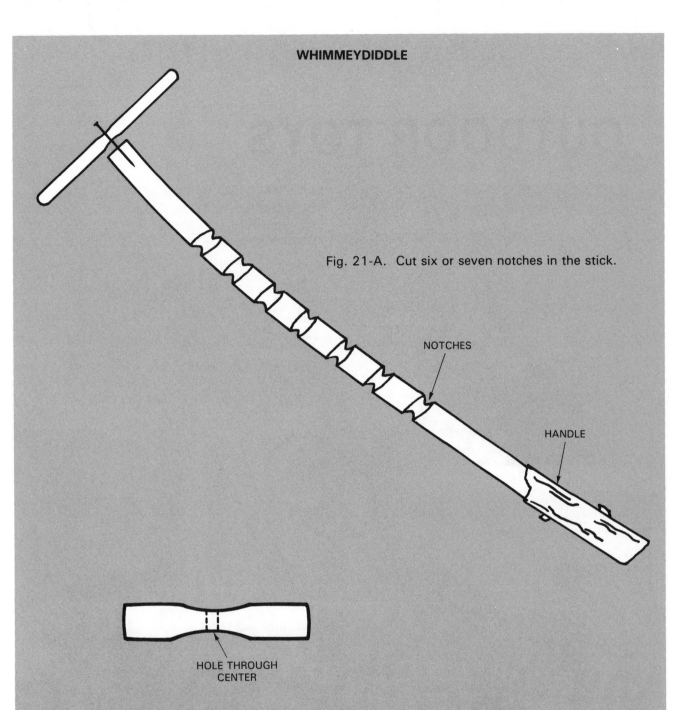

Fig. 21-A. Cut six or seven notches in the stick.

NOTCHES

HANDLE

HOLE THROUGH
CENTER

Fig. 21-B. Shaping rotor and drilling hole through
center.

OUTDOOR TOYS

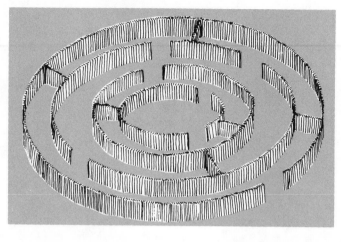

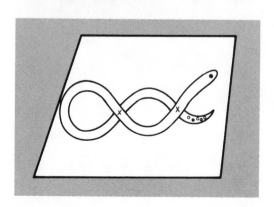

Boats

Around 1900, the family laundry was done in large tin washtubs. On a hot summer day, a tub of water would be set in the backyard to be heated. Hours of fun then began for small inland sailors.

Boats held a fascination for youngsters in those days. Children made simple ones from discarded odds and ends. With wood from an orange crate or cigar box, rubber bands, a bit of camphor, and a bar of Ivory soap, they had the "makings" of a fleet.

PADDLEWHEEL BOAT

CAMPHOR BOAT

SOAP SAILBOAT

PADDLEWHEEL BOAT

Supplies: For body and paddles, 1 piece balsa or basswood, 9'' x 3'' x 3/16''; several rubber bands, 2 in. long, (spares needed); waterproof glue; fine sandpaper.

53

Tools: Craft knife.

How to make
1. Cut body and two paddles out of wood, Fig. 22-A. Sand edges.
2. Slide paddles together to form the paddlewheel. They will interlock at right angles. Glue where paddles join.
3. Place the rubber band across the back of the body fitting it in the notches as shown in Fig. 22-B. Insert two adjacent paddles of the paddlewheel through the rubber band so it cannot slide out.

To use, wind up the rubber band by turning the paddlewheel. Place the boat in the water. Release the paddlewheel.

CAMPHOR BOAT

Supplies and tools: One piece, balsa wood, 4 1/2'' x 2 1/2'' x 3/16''; lump of camphor from drug store; fine sandpaper; craft knife.

How to make
1. Cut body of boat out of balsa. Sand edges as in Fig. 22-C.
2. To power the boat, place a lump of camphor in the notch on back of boat.
3. Place the boat in the water.

SOAP SAILBOAT

Supplies and tools: Bar of soap that floats; small sheet of typing paper for sail; waterproof glue; round wooden toothpick; scissors.

How to make
1. Make a paper sail. Fold edge on the fold line. Glue it around the toothpick, Fig. 22-D.
2. Stick end of the toothpick into the soap.

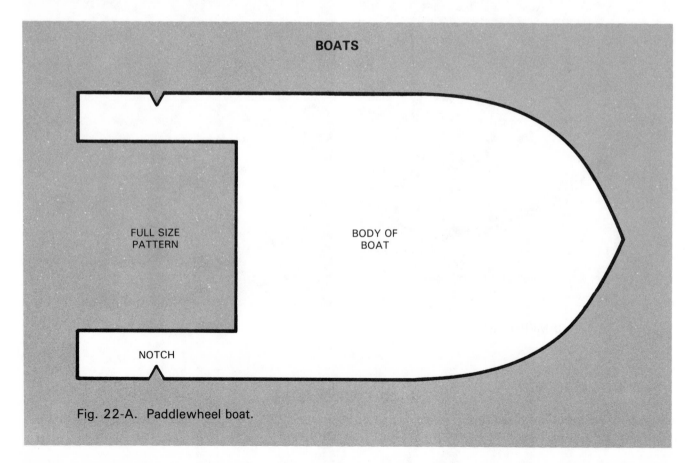

Fig. 22-A. Paddlewheel boat.

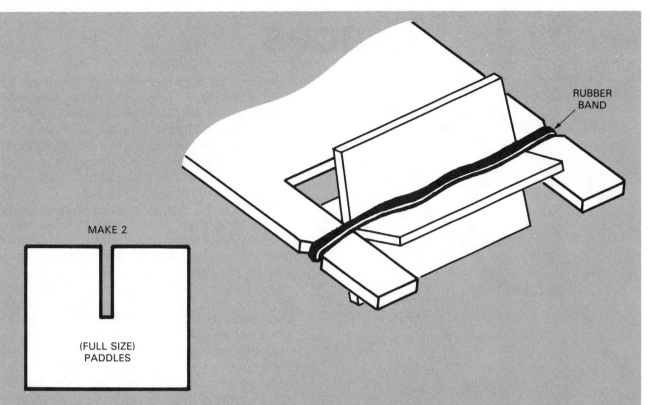

RUBBER
BAND

MAKE 2

(FULL SIZE)
PADDLES

Fig. 22-B. Attaching rubber band and paddle
(not to scale).

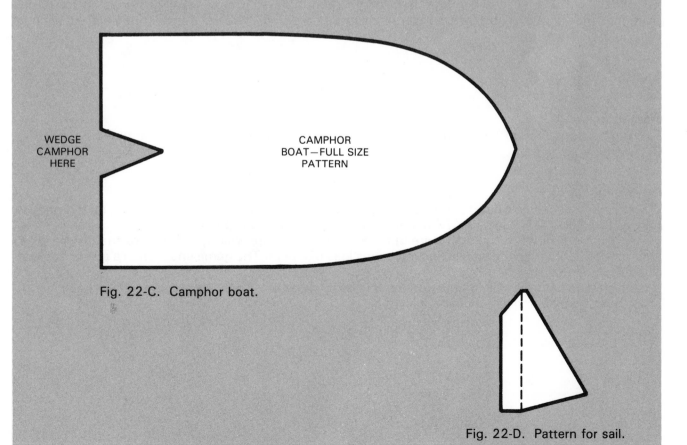

WEDGE
CAMPHOR
HERE

CAMPHOR
BOAT—FULL SIZE
PATTERN

Fig. 22-C. Camphor boat.

Fig. 22-D. Pattern for sail.

Graces

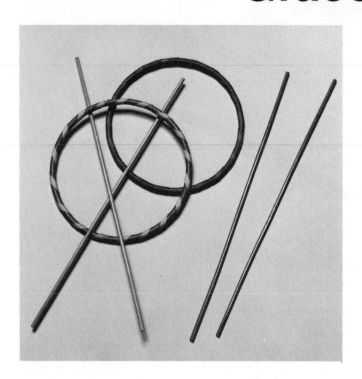

Parents considered this hoop game an outdoor exercise in feminine grace. Therefore, proper young Victorian ladies were likely to be found playing Graces on a summer day.

Each player held two 18 inch sticks and a lightweight wooden hoop about 10 inches in diameter. The hoops might have been decorated with ribbons or tinsel.

To start the game, two opposing players would hang their hoops over crossed sticks. Then by quickly moving the sticks apart, they sent the hoops flying toward the other player. The object was to catch the hoop over the sticks and return it. The hoops were kept moving back and forth until one player missed. Each miss cost a point. The first player to lose all of her points lost the game.

At one time it was considered barely acceptable for boys to play Graces. A book on outdoor games for boys, written after the Civil war, cautions them to play the game only indoors and never with another boy!

Supplies: Two 1/4 in. dowels, standard length (about 31 in.); two wooden hoops, 8 to 10 in. diameter (these are available where macrame supplies are sold); two yd. narrow ribbon (1 yd. each of two colors); white glue.

Tools: Saw or knife.

How to make
1. Wind ribbons around hoops. Use a different color on each hoop. Secure with glue.
2. Saw dowels in half.

Playing the game
Each player receives a hoop and two sticks. Cross the sticks with the hoop hanging on the narrow part of the "X," as in Fig. 23-A. Players start the game with 20 points each.

The game starts when the sticks are moved apart. The hoops will fly off toward the other player who tries to catch it on the sticks. Failure means loss of a point The game ends when a player has lost all points.

Until players become skilled at the game, it is best to use one hoop. Later, each player has a hoop. They must be exchanged simultaneously.

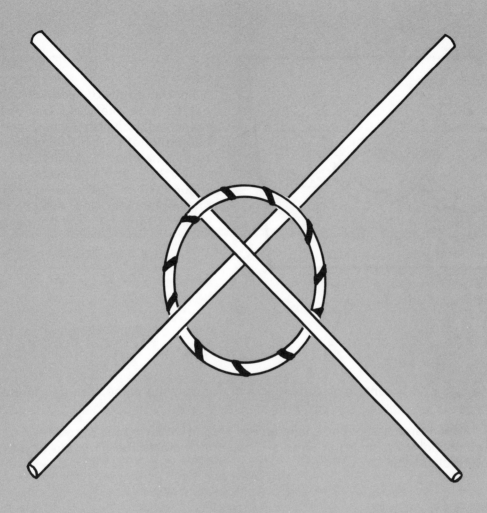

Fig. 23-A. How to hold the hoop.

Serpent

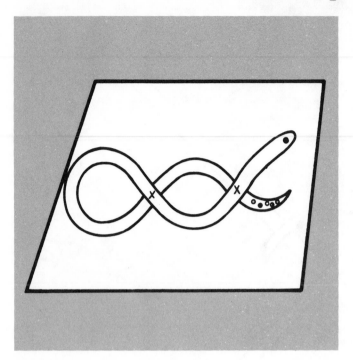

For thousands of years, children have played games with marbles. The children of early French and English settlers and the sons and daughters of British troops brought this game to the American Colonies.

In 1921, archaeologists working on a site thought to be the remains of an early English encampment in New Albany, discovered the outline of this game in the hard packed earth.

Supplies: Marbles of different colors; pointed stick for drawing game area on ground.

Preparation: Draw a large serpentine shape on the ground following the pattern in Fig. 24-A. Mark in the Xs at intersections but omit the arrows. They only indicate the direction of play. Scoop out a small diameter hole at the "eye."

To play
1. Each player selects a different color of marble.
2. Each player shoots selected marble over the game area in the direction of play indicated in Fig. 24-A. The shot is taken from the tail. Each player's marble is left where it lands. (There are different methods for "shooting" the marble. One way is shown in Fig. 24-B. A flick of the thumb will propel the marble with considerable force.)
3. Play continues in rotation until one player rolls his or her marble into the eye of the serpent.

Penalties
1. Any marble rolling outside the lines of the serpent's body must go back to the starting line (tail) and start over.
2. Any marble struck by another must go back to the tail and begin again.
3. Any marble landing on an X loses a turn.

Fig. 24-A. Arrows show direction of play.

Fig. 24-B. How to hold marble for shooting.

Corn Husk Ball

An ear of corn provided hours of entertainment for youngsters in the frontier days. Using either the husks or cob after the kernels were removed, a girl would be likely to make a doll. Boys made balls from the husks. The balls were remarkably sturdy.

Supplies: About 10 dry corn husks; cotton string, 3 yd.; styrofoam ball, 1 1/2 in. dia., for core.

Tools: Scissors.

Making the ball
1. Soak corn husks in warm water 20 to 30 minutes. Drain off water and roll husks in a towel.
2. Soak the string in water. It will shrink as it dries making a tighter ball of husks.
3. Tear the husks lengthwise into 1 in. wide strips. Corn husks always tear straight.
4. To save drying time, use a styrofoam ball as the core. Wrap husks around the ball, covering the end of the preceding husk with the tip of the new one. Wrap in all directions to keep the ball round.
5. Finish off the ball by wrapping string around it in all directions keeping the string taut. When the husks are secured, tie off the string.
6. Allow ball to dry overnight before using.

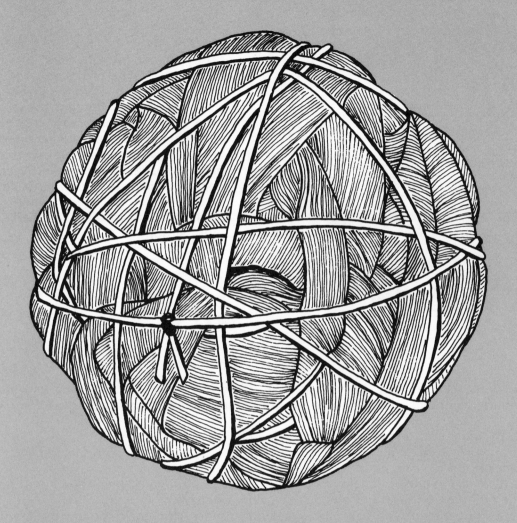

Ball of corn husks. Wetting string before wrapping will
make the ball tighter since string will shrink as it dries.

Ben Franklin Kite

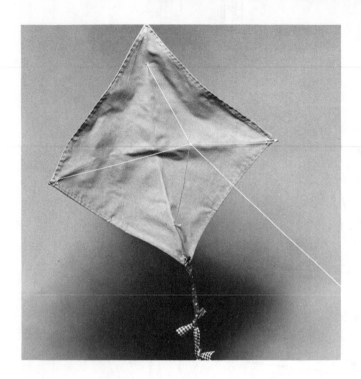

Boys of early America had a traditional cycle of sports. A time of the year was devoted to each amusement. With the first sign of Spring, the cycle began. The first season was marble time, followed in succession by tops and kites.

A few fancy kites were imported from China but most boys made their own. Cedar, spruce or fir was used for the sticks. The cover was of paper or linen. If linen was used, the maker smeared it with linseed oil after the kite was made. The oil stiffened the fabric and made it more airtight.

Supplies: Unbleached muslin, 19 in. sq.; two 24 in. bamboo balloon sticks; kite string; needle, thread, and straight pins; boiled linseed oil; rectangular scraps of calico about 1'' x 10''

Tools: Craft knife; scissors; brush for spreading oil

How to make
1. Make 1/2'' slit in ends of sticks. Find middle of sticks and lash them together at right angles.
2. Tie the string onto the end of one stick leaving a 6 in. end.
3. Run the string through slits of all sticks making a frame. After going through a slit, wrap the string around the stock to secure it. Then move on to the next slit. Continue around the sticks to the starting point. Go through the first slit again and tie the string off. Keep the frame square. See Fig. 26-A.
4. Lay the frame down on the material. Draw around it so that there will be enough material for an inch hem. Cut on the line. Fold the hem over the string and pin in place. Sew hem as close to the string as possible.
5. Lay the kite material front side up on white paper. Brush on linseed oil. Let it dry.
6. The bridle strings are attached to the front of the kite. Make tiny holes to pass them through the material. Tie the strings around the sticks. The string on the ''north-south'' stick should be 36 in. long. The string on the ''east-west'' stick should be about 24 in. long. It is tied about 4 in. in from the ends of the stick. See sketch in Fig. 26-B.
7. Put a finger under the intersection of the bridle strings. Hold at a 20 degree angle to the floor. Tie flying string here.
8. Make the tail by tying strips of calico together until you have a tail 20 times the length of the kite. Attach it to the kite at the south tip. Test the kite. The tail can be lengthened or shortened as needed.

BEN FRANKLIN KITE

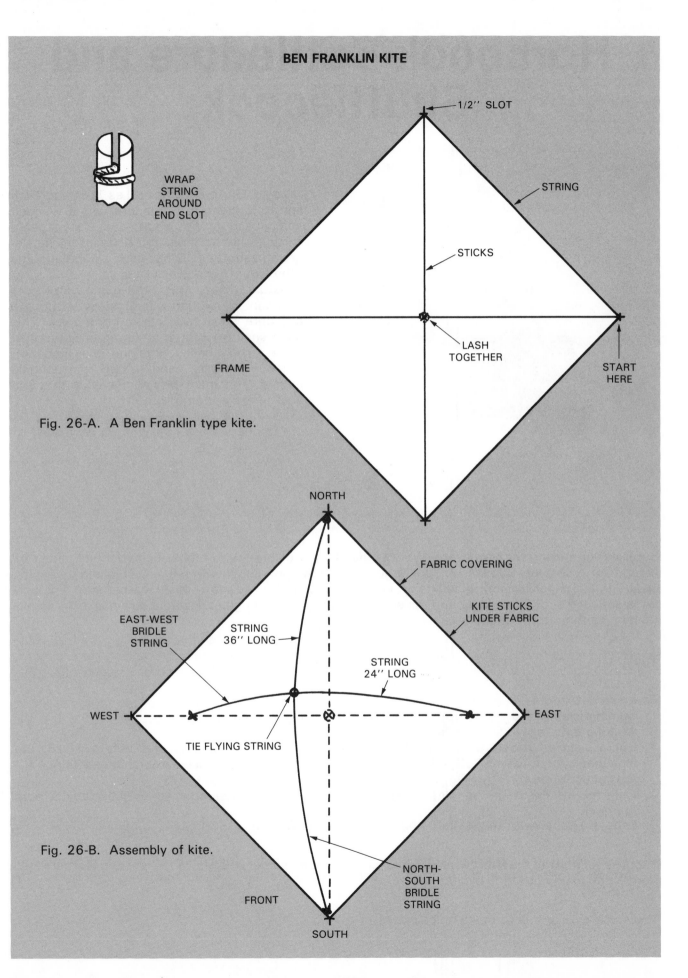

WRAP
STRING
AROUND
END SLOT

1/2'' SLOT

STRING

STICKS

LASH
TOGETHER

FRAME

START
HERE

Fig. 26-A. A Ben Franklin type kite.

NORTH

FABRIC COVERING

KITE STICKS
UNDER FABRIC

EAST-WEST
BRIDLE
STRING

STRING
36'' LONG

STRING
24'' LONG

WEST

EAST

TIE FLYING STRING

Fig. 26-B. Assembly of kite.

NORTH-
SOUTH
BRIDLE
STRING

FRONT

SOUTH

Hornbook Battledore and Shuttlecock

In colonial America as well as 16th and 17th century England, a battledore was a wooden paddle used to bat shuttlecocks in a game similar to lawn tennis and badminton. Battledore and shuttlecock has been a popular game in the Orient for 2000 years.

Boston stores carried the game before the American Revolution. Youngsters without a battledore substituted their hornbooks. This was a sheet of vellum mounted on a wooden paddle. The sheet contained the alphabet, Roman numerals, and other instructional material. The sheet was overlayed with a thin cover of transparent horn.

The shuttlecock was easy to make. A cork with feathers stuck in it worked very well.

Supplies for making the battledore: Wooden paddle toy of type with rubber ball attached; sheet of parchment type paper (you can antique regular paper by sponging it with tea or coffee and drying it); clear contact paper for horn; fine-line brown marking pen; brown shoe polish; leather strip 1/2 inch wide and long enough to go around the edge of the paper; white glue; dozen or so small tacks for attaching leather strip; sandpaper.

Tools: tack hammer; scissors; drill.

To make battledore
1. Remove elastic and staple from the paddle. Sand off any markings.
2. Antique with brown shoe polish. Remove excess polish.
3. Cut a piece of paper for the hornbook lesson. Since this hornbook dates before 1818, the alphabet will not have a ''J'' or ''U'' in it. At that time ''I'' and ''J'' were interchangeable. A ''V'' was substituted for ''U,'' Fig. 27-A.
4. Glue the lesson on the paddle. Cover it with the clear contact paper as a substitute for horn material.
5. Edge the paper with the leather strip. Tack it in place.

Supplies for making the shuttlecock: Cork ball 2 inches in diameter; eight to ten chicken feathers (get from a craft shop or farm); white glue.

Tools: Ice pick or tool to make holes in ball.

To make shuttlecock

1. Punch a hole in the ball for each feather. Make them in a cluster. See Fig. 27-B.
2. Press stems of feathers into the holes. (You can glue them in place if you wish.)

HORNBOOK BATTLEDORE, AND SHUTTLECOCK

Fig. 27-A. Sample lettering for hornbook.

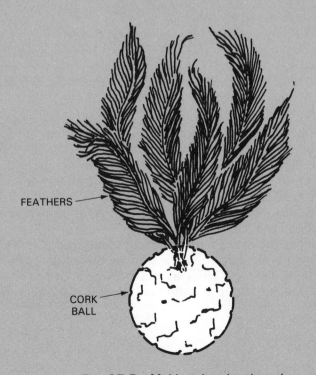

FEATHERS

CORK
BALL

Fig. 27-B. Making the shuttlecock.

MAZE

St. Lammas Day, celebrated on August 1, was traditionally a day of thanksgiving. It signaled the beginning of the harvest season.

On that day, the first fruits of the harvest were brought to the churches to be blessed.

Following the ceremony the community feasted and played games.

While their parents sat at the harvest table and watched, children often played in a maze constructed for the occasion. Usually the walls of the maze were built from sheaves of grain or from clumps of sod that had been turned up in a pattern of circular walkways and passages. Smaller versions were often carved in wood or drawn on paper.

St. Lammas Day was celebrated both in England and on the Continent from early Christian times. The English called the church service a "loaf mass" while on the Continent it was referred to as the "lamb's mass." American settlers brought the tradition with them. Until 1863, when Abraham Lincoln declared Thanksgiving a national holiday, each community had a time for its own thanksgiving festival. The date elected was August 1 or Lammas Day.

In the late 17th century the Puritans became concerned over the running of the maze. It had become such a fad that they banned it in an attempt to suppress "those folyshe ceremonies".

Supplies: Powdered chalk, rope, or bales of straw for walls; yardstick or stick cut to size.

To make
1. Plan the maze on paper. It may be any size or shape. In the old days, children might have had to walk half a mile to reach the center.
2. Start planning from the center. Draw a wall around it. In the wall place an opening as in Fig. 28-A.
3. Draw a second wall around the first with a path between them. Put a door in this wall and a wall across the path to block it, Fig. 28-B.
4. Continue adding walls, paths, and openings until the maze is the size you want. Fig. 28-C shows a small completed maze.
5. When making the maze outdoors, use chalk, rope, or bales of straw for the walls. To keep the width of the paths uniform, cut a stick to the width of the path wanted. Mark the innermost wall surrounding the center. Then lay the stick against the wall. The end of the stick provides a marking guide. Move it along the old wall as you mark each new wall, Fig. 28-D.

MAZE

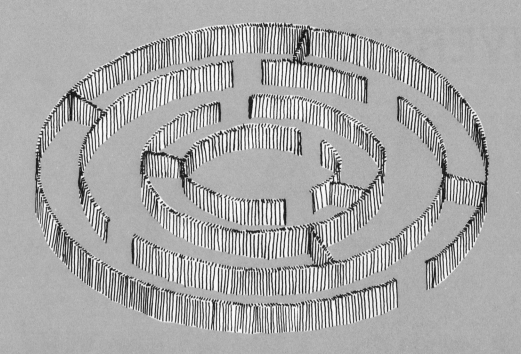

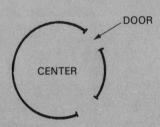

Fig. 28-A. Start of maze.

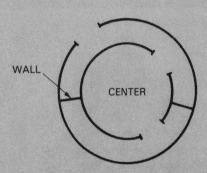

Fig. 28-B. Adding walls and barriers.

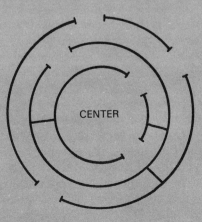

Fig. 28-C. Maze completed.

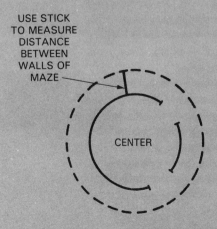

Fig. 28-D. Using measuring stick.

DIVERSIONS

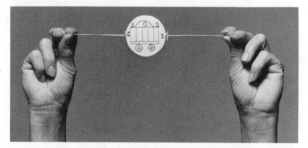

Noah's Ark

Parents' strict observance of the Sabbath could make Sunday a dreary day for children of early America. The only exception to the ban on entertainment was the Noah's Ark toy. Its biblical connection made it acceptable.

There were as many different styles of arks as there were makers. However, they did share some characteristics. In all of them, a rectangular house sat atop a small boat. The roof lifted off so that all its passengers could be set inside. Often, the house was decorated to resemble the home of the child.

The originator of the ark is unknown but we do know that it came out of Germany early in the 17th century. Until the 1890s, the ark and its inhabitants were fashioned from wood. Then, when paper toys became popular as advertising giveaways, a Connecticut thread company offered Noah's Arks. The animals, too, were paper cutouts with an easel back. A verse, printed on the reverse of each animal, advertised the company's thread.

Supplies for a Noah's Ark: One piece of basswood, 12'' x 8'' x 3/16''; two strips of balsa, 9'' x 1/2'' x 1/32''; model enamel or acrylic paints; white glue; black laundry marking pen; brown shoe polish, paste type; tracing paper and soft pencil; string or rubber bands; fine sandpaper.

Tools: Craft knife; metal edge ruler; brushes for paint and glue.

To make

1. Trace patterns, (twice where two of a kind are needed). Turn penciled side down on basswood. Retrace to transfer patterns. See Figs. 29-A, 29-B, and 29-C.
2. Cut out all the parts. Score the lines with the point of a knife. Use the ruler as a guide for straight lines. Cut away excess wood. Sand edges.
3. Paint all the pieces. Outline details with the laundry pen when the paint is dry.
4. Soak the 1/2 in. strips of balsa in warm water.
5. Working on wax paper, glue both sides of the building, Fig. 29-D, to one end piece. Check corners for right angles. Butt the sides onto one end of the building. Glue on the other end. See pattern, Fig. 29-C. Again, check corner angles. Clamp by putting a rubber band around the building while the glue dries.
6. Remove the 1/2'' strips of balsa from the water. Blot them with a towel. They should be ready to shape to the deck. Starting in the middle of one curved end, shape them around the deck, (Fig. 29-A). Hold in place with string or rubber bands and allow them to dry.
7. Lay a protective strip of wax paper over the top edges of the building. Form the roof by putting glue on sloped edges of the ends and assembling the roof pieces (Fig. 29-B) on top of the building. Butt the short piece against the long one. Clamp until dry. Do not glue the roof onto building. It must lift off!
8. When the balsa strips dry, glue them onto the edge of the deck. Clamp them once more.

9. Give an antique look to both deck and building by rubbing with shoe polish. Buff with a clean cloth, if you wish.
10. Glue building to deck. Sign and date the ark. You have made an heirloom.
11. Animals can be purchased, carved from wood, made with paper or molded from plaster—any way you wish.

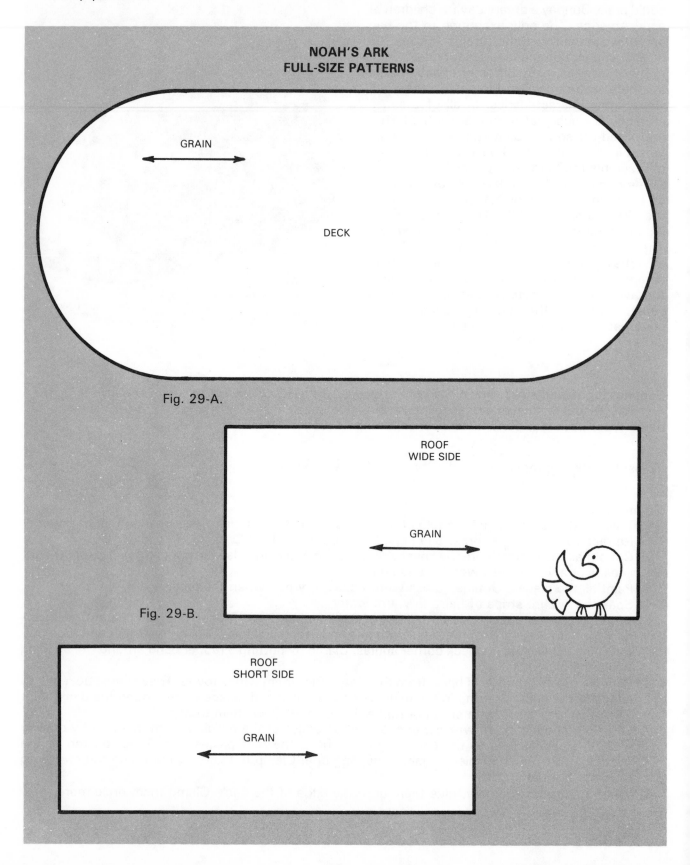

**NOAH'S ARK
FULL-SIZE PATTERNS**

GRAIN

DECK

Fig. 29-A.

ROOF
WIDE SIDE

GRAIN

Fig. 29-B.

ROOF
SHORT SIDE

GRAIN

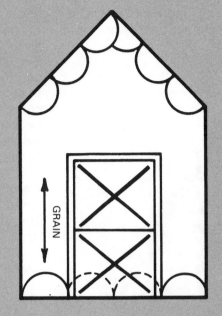

MAKE TWO BUILDING
ENDS. ONE HAS DOOR;
OTHER HAS WINDOW.

GRAIN

Fig. 29-C.

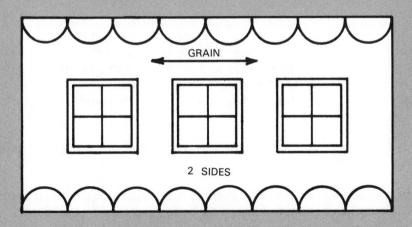

GRAIN

2 SIDES

Fig. 29-D.

Victorian Peep Show

A peep show is a miniature scene created in a closed box. Depending upon the scene, it may be lighted from the side, top, or bottom.

The viewer looks through a small hole in one end.

The peep show has a long, fascinating history. The first ones go back to the Renaissance when craftspeople and artists experimented with three-dimensional perspectives. They were used by the early Christian churches to illustrate Bible stories for illiterate peasants. The scenes were set up in large mobile cabinets which could be taken from fair to fair.

By the 17th century, much smaller ones were being made. An ingenious method of painting scenes on mica slides was developed. The slides fit into slots inside the box. The large shows continued to be popular at fairs in the 18th century but the subject matter changed from biblical to historical events.

Victorians, inspired by interest in optical toys, devised the ultimate peep show. The shape became triangular and was lined with mirrors.

Peep shows are, perhaps, the best of all toys. They are as much fun for the maker as for the viewer.

Supplies: Piece of heavy mat board, 13 by 13 inches; two mirrors, 3 by 6 inches (have them cut where mirrors are sold, they are very inexpensive); odds and ends to make a scene in the peep show: moss, two or three tiny figures and a few dried flowers (they will be reflected by mirrors and made to look like more); masking tape; white glue; white gesso; acrylic or model enamel paints; one piece, white construction paper; watercolor paints.

Tools: Craft knife; ruler; protractor; clip clothespins; tweezers; brushes for paint and glue.

To make
1. See Fig. 30-A for layout of peep show box. Dimensions are indicated. Draw on cardboard.
2. Cut out the peep show. Score base triangle lines with knife. Cut out the peephole.
3. Decide on scene for peep show.
4. Draw outline of Side A on construction paper. Paint a sky on it with watercolors. Dry. Glue it to Side A.
5. Glue mirrors on Sides B and C. Clamp with clothespins until the glue dries.
6. Glue grass and other chosen materials onto the base triangle. This will be the floor of the show.
7. Fold sides A, B, and C along scored lines to form a box with a triangular shape. Be sure the mirrors butt together. Hole the outside corners together with masking tape.
8. Paint the outside of the box and upper edges with gesso. Let it dry and, then, paint with enamel.
9. Put an object in the peep show. Move it around to study the multiple images. The reflections of the peep hole can be blocked by the manner in which the scene is arranged.
10. Glue the scene in place when the arrangement suits your fancy.

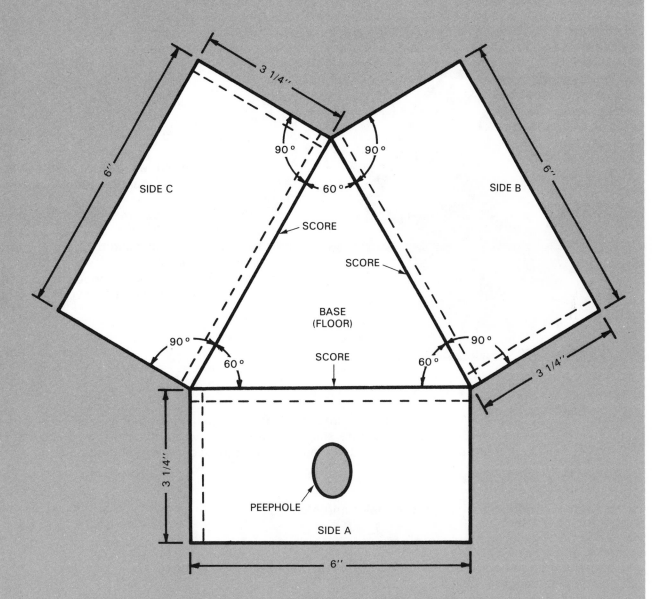

Fig. 30-A. Peep show box to half scale (1/2'' = 1'').

Picture Puzzle Blocks

Whether they were imported from Europe or made by the local carpenter, blocks were a popular toy of early American children. Many blocks were adorned with letters, numbers, or part of pictures. It is possible that many immigrants, lacking an education themselves, favored these educational type blocks for their children.

Shortly before the American Revolution, sets of picture puzzle blocks were imported from Holland. A set consisted of six or more blocks with a part of a different picture on each side. They could be arranged to make six different pictures with the box serving as the frame.

Supplies: Piece of lumber 1'' x 4'' x 4'' or any dimension that will yield nine 1 inch cubes; six illustrations 3 inches square (read instructions before selecting them); heavy cardboard 6 inches square; white glue; masking tape; model enamel or acrylic paint for box; gesso; wax paper; scrap cardboard 4 inches square.

Tools: Craft knife; brushes for applying paint and glue; ruler.

To make
1. Sand lumber and cut it into 1 inch cubes. You will need nine of them.
2. Sand sawed edges of blocks.
3. Make a template of the scrap cardboard for selecting pictures. Cut a 3 inch square opening in it.
4. Lay the template over large pictures selected from magazines or other sources. Move the template over different areas of the picture and select a portion you like.
5. Draw cutting lines on the picture with the template.
6. Select and mark six pictures in this fashion and cut them out.
7. Work with one picture at a time. Lay the picture face down on a piece of wax paper.
8. Brush a thin coat of glue over the back of the picture.
9. Lay the blocks on it to cover it entirely.
10. Carefully, turn the assembly right side up. Smooth the picture and let the glue dry.
11. Cut blocks apart with a craft knife. You will be able to use the indentations between blocks as a cutting guide. Repeat steps 8 through 11 with the other pictures.
12. Make a box to hold the blocks using the 6 inch square of cardboard. Assemble the blocks on the cardboard. Center the assembly and draw a line along each edge. See Fig. 31-A.
13. Cut flaps at corners and fold up the sides to form a box. Hold the corners together with glue and masking tape. Use tape to reinforce the bottom folds, also.

14. Paint the box with gesso. When the gesso is dry, paint the box with enamel.
15. Coat all sides of each block with white glue to protect the pictures. The glue will dry clear.

Using the picture blocks
Use the box as a frame when attempting to assemble the different picture puzzles.

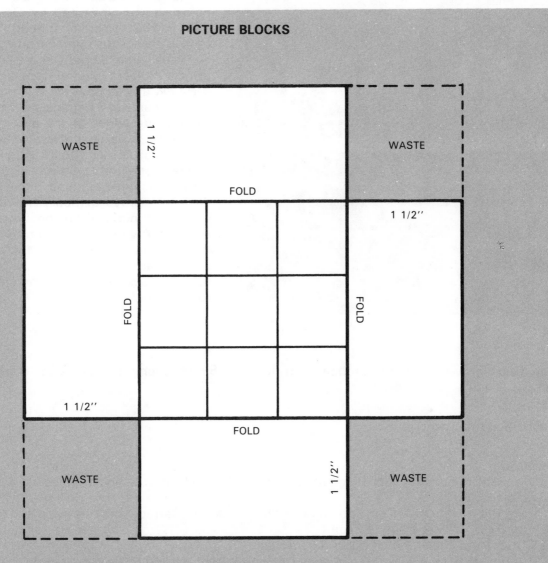

Fig. 31-A. Marking and cutting cardboard box.

Thaumatrope

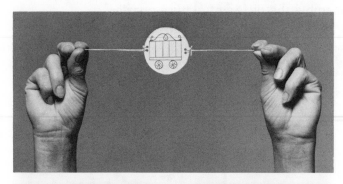

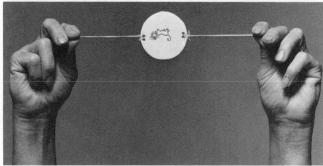

The thaumatrope is a small toy with a big name. It was invented by Dr. John Ayrton Paris in 1825 to prove a theory. He wanted an optical device to demonstrate that what the eye sees persists briefly as a visual image even after the object is gone from sight.

He did this by drawing two different images on either side of a paper disk. Strings were tied to opposite edges of the disk. When the strings were rotated between the fingers, the disk could be made to twirl rapidly. The two images appeared to be one picture.

Dr. Paris' invention may have been a serious device to prove a theory but, for a while, it became a popular toy on both sides of the Atlantic. A variation sometimes seen is to cast the disk in metal and mount it with pivot pins into a hand-held bracket. Flicking the forefinger across the edge of the disk causes it to rotate rapidly.

Supplies: Lightweight white cardboard; string about 8 inches long; thin black line marking pen; tracing paper and soft lead pencil.

Tools: Scissors; paper punch.

To make
1. Trace the entire design including the outside of the circle and the holes. Holes will serve as register marks. See Fig. 32-A.
2. Turn the tracing pencil side down onto the cardboard. Retrace only the cage and hole markings, Fig. 32-B. Do not trace the lion.
3. Cut out the circle. Punch holes for the string.
4. Turn the disk over. Using the original tracing, retrace the lion upside down onto the disk. See Fig. 32-C. Be sure to line up outline of holes on the tracing with punched holes.
5. Go over the drawings with a marker.
6. Tie a 4 inch string through each hole of the disk.
7. Fig. 32-D is a design for another thaumatrope. Place the outline on the jack-o-lantern on one side of the disk, the features on the other side.

To make it work
Hold the strings taut between the thumb and forefinger of each hand. Roll the string back and forth between the thumbs and forefingers. The disk will whirl first in one direction, then in the other.

Fig. 32-A. Pattern.

HOLE
FOR STRING

Fig. 32-B. Trace wagon on front of disk.

Fig. 32-C. Trace lion on back of disk.

Fig. 32-D. Alternate pattern.

Scissor Toy

The popularity of scissor toys, first noted in the age of the Renaissance, endures to the modern plastic age. Although variations abound, the basic design has remained unchanged. Thin slats of wood are hinged to each other so they act like a series of levers. When the two slats at one end are squeezed, the other end, to which a small figure is attached, will dart away. Opening the two levers will retract the figure.

Older examples of this toy were pegged together with small wooden figures that appeared to march back and forth as the framework was opened and closed. When the toy was "Americanized," pegs were substituted for the wooden figures. Handles and a ghost doll were added.

The ability of the toy to expand rapidly in length makes it a perfect Halloween toy. It has been used to startle many an unwary victim.

Supplies: Balsa or basswood, 12" x 3" x 3/16"; styrofoam ball, 2 in. diameter; 16 brass headed paper fasteners with 1/2 in. legs; black model enamel; cheese cloth, 9 by 18 in.; string; black felt scraps for eyes; 2 straight pins with white bead heads; white glue; scrap cardboard for patterns; fine sandpaper.

Tools: Craft knife; metal edge ruler; scissors.

How to make
1. Make cardboard patterns of Figs. 33-A through 33-D. Use them to draw parts on wood. Cut out all parts. Use the metal edged ruler when cutting straight lines with the craft knife.
2. Sand edges.
3. Paint all pieces black.
4. Assemble scissor part of toy as shown in Fig. 33-F. Insert paper fasteners through the holes to hold parts together. Paint heads of fasteners with black enamel.
5. Impale the ball on the pointed end of the assembly (Fig. 33-D). Double the cheese cloth to make a 9 in. square. Drape the cloth over the ball in a ghostly manner. Secure the ball with a piece of string. Glue on black felt eyes. Insert bead-headed pins as eyes, Fig. 33-E.

To use
To make the ghost jump back and forth, open and close the assembled toy using the handles like a scissors.

SCISSOR TOY

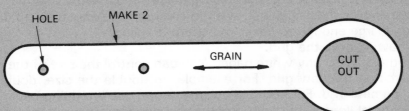

Fig. 33-A. Pattern for handle.

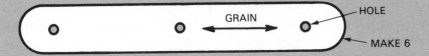

Fig. 33-B. Pattern for scissor parts.

Fig. 33-C. Pattern for scissors.

Fig. 33-D. Pattern for scissors.

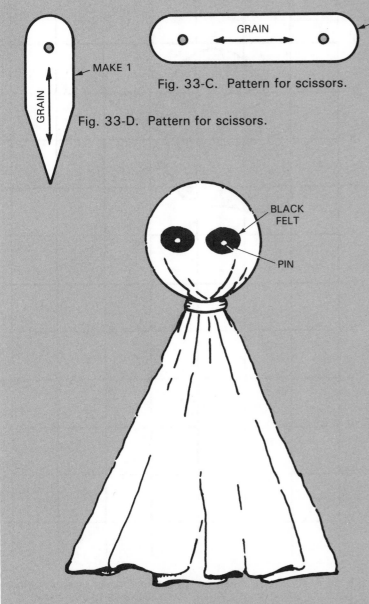

Fig. 33-E. Attaching eyes to "ghost."

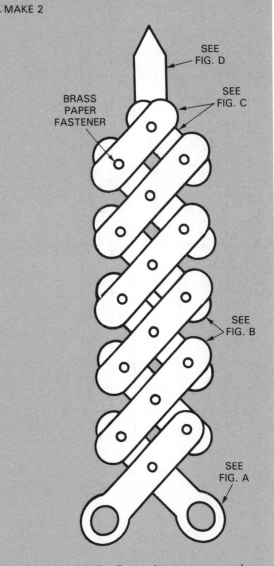

Fig. 33-F. Fastening parts together.

HOW TO ENLARGE OR REDUCE A PATTERN

Toy patterns, such as the Sawyers or the Climbing Bear, can be enlarged or reduced by the simple "squares" method. To enlarge a design follow these simple steps:

1. Lay off squares over the design you wish to enlarge. You may want to do this on tracing paper. Make the grid large enough to cover the entire drawing.
2. Trace the drawing onto the grid.
3. Prepare another grid on any white paper. You can control the size of the enlargement by the size of the squares on the new grid. For example, to double the size, double the size of individual squares in the new grid. For very big enlargements, use wrapping paper.
4. Number horizontal lines in the grids from top to bottom. Letter vertical lines from left to right.
5. Mark the points on the enlarged grid where pattern lines cross the vertical and horizontal lines.
6. Join the points of intersection working freehand. A French curve may be used to produce smooth, rounded curves.
7. Trace your pattern on your material either by flopping and retracing or by using carbon paper between the pattern and your material.
8. To reduce a pattern simply make the new grid smaller than the original.

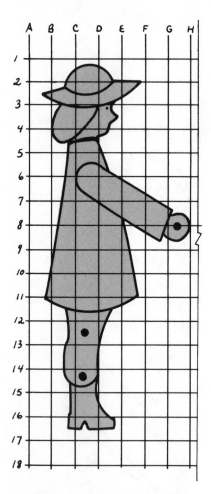

LAY OFF SQUARES OVER THE ORIGINAL
DESIGN AND TRACE THE DRAWING
ONTO THE GRID.

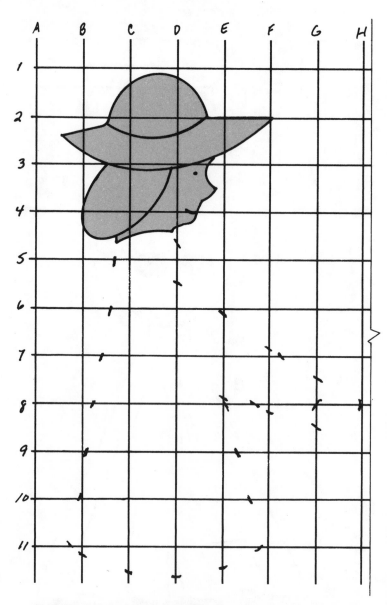

PREPARE ANOTHER GRID OF THE SIZE YOU WANT NEW PATTERN
TO BE. MARK POINTS WHERE PATTERN LINES CROSS THE GRID
LINES. CONNECT PARTS WITH FREEHAND PATTERN LINES.